Folklore, Legends and Spells

By the same author
An English Rose

SELENA IBBOTT

Folklore, Legends and Spells

Ashgrove Press, Bath

Published in Great Britain by
ASHGROVE PRESS LIMITED
7 Locksbrook Road Estate
Bath, BA1 3DZ

ISBN 1–85398–034–X

First published 1994

Typeset by
Ann Buchan (Typesetters),Middlesex
Printed in England by
Redwood Books, Trowbridge

For my mother Carole, and in memory of my Grandfather Arthur Samuel Upham, who was, still is and always will be the most influential person in my life.

Acknowledgements

Firstly thanks must go to my family. My mother for her patience, advice, loving support and for always being there when I needed her. My father for endless supplies of stationery for which without typing would be an impossible task! My grandmothers for allowing me to pick their brains at every given opportunity, and for sharing with me their childhood memories and 'wisdom'. Friends and neighbours of the past and present who unbeknowingly, through the ancient art of conversation gave me countless superstitions, legends, old sayings and other snippets of information of interest to me. My sister Helen who undertook my leg work and helped with research. Finally, a big thank you to my friend and healer – Patricia Hurrell who eased away the pain of 'writer's neck'.

My sincere thanks to the following; The Bristol & Gloucestershire Archaeological Society. The staff of Dursley, Gloucester and Evesham Library. Barbara Griffiths from the Gloucester Historical Library. Mrs F. Handcock and Mr Dennis Forbs (Cambridge University Press, Cambridge) who assisted me without any hesitation.

Alan Sutton from Alan Sutton Publishing for help in the past when this book was merely a pipe dream before writing *An English Rose*; for never refusing me help when I needed it – Thank you.

John Huges. I am indebted to you. Never a question was left unanswered, every phone call was returned, every letter replied.

Graham J. Stockham (Gloucestershire Rural Community Council. For permission to quote from the Gloucestershire W.I. Records 1850–1950.

Mr John Humphries – owner of the Ancient Ram Inn & Mr P. Harris. Author J.A. Brooks: Author and friend Karl Francis for tips on numerology.

My thanks to Mrs H. Grove and Gillian Entwistle for information on local legends. Gizmo – for your love, loyalty and friendship.

Rose & Bill Williams, Mary & Pat and Rosemary Williams; friends in spirit . . . your memories live on through the pages of this book.

Contents

Foreword

Growing up around my grandparents and elderly people gave me the opportunity to observe, listen and acquire knowledge, without which I couldn't even attempt to write about traditions, herbs, folklore and superstitions. I was a very curious, persistent, direct child, with a burning desire to know everything, and I wouldn't take no for an answer. My grandfather used to say that I had: 'the face of an angel and the cheek of the Devil.' But at the same time I was respectful, helpful, and considerate to my elders. It was this combination which enabled me to acquire the information which had always interested me from an early age, and it has remained with me to this day, as have the memories of the people whom I would sit and talk to for hours as a child, especially those who have now passed over into spirit.

My interest in herbs and folklore stems from my mother, who, over the years, has shared both her love and knowledge of herbs with me. At the age of thirteen, much to my mother's delight, I began to show great enthusiasm in her much-loved hobby, herbalism. But unlike my mother, I was more intrigued and fascinated by the superstitions connected with herbs and other plants alike, which for centuries have been associated with witchcraft, and still hold a certain aura of magic today.

I have tried to gather together in this book a wide variety of folklore, wives'-tales, old sayings, and superstitions. I have given the reasons behind the superstitions whenever possible, and in places given my own personal views and beliefs, which some of you may find strange. Transferring the legends and spells to a typed script from old books, memory, word of mouth and information scribbled down on endless pieces of paper scattered all around the place was the most challenging and enjoyable part of all.

It has been both interesting and fun researching and compiling this book, and I am more than happy to share my findings with you. I hope that you have as much pleasure reading this book as I had writing it. And remember, the superstitions within these pages are not to be taken too seriously, but to avoid any bad luck, tap the book three times before reading it!

S.I.

Introduction

We can govern our fate, control our own destinies, predict the future, adhere to superstition, or choose to cast it aside and totally ignore it. Those who regard superstition as old 'hocus-pocus' do in fact subconsciously carry out some kind of superstitious act daily, but are unaware of it on a conscious level. Stepping aside on the stairs to allow the other person to pass, avoiding walking underneath ladders, and making sure that knives never cross when setting the table for dinner, are three of the most common superstitions of significance which are undertaken daily by hundreds of people all over the world from all walks of life.

Do you carry a lucky charm? Many people do, but won't admit it. People wear or carry all manner of things, from a bent silver coin to a rabbit's foot which they are convinced bring them good luck. The object itself, whatever it may be, is irrelevant. It's the power, faith, and belief of the owner which makes the charm lucky. And how many of you think twice before opening an umbrella indoors, or putting a new pair of shoes on the kitchen table? These are just two well known examples. Whether you are superstitious or not you would have, at one time or another, thought twice before doing something for fear of attracting bad luck.

My pet hate is people who do take notice of superstition but claim that they're not in the least superstitious. Such people usually say something like: 'I don't really believe in it, it's all a lot of nonsense!' But they still continue to read their daily horoscope. They may just quickly glance at it, and then think no more of it, that is until an event takes place which coincides with what they have read, then they start to wonder whether or not there *is* some truth in it after all!

I didn't realise until writing this book just how much superstition influenced me as a child. Many pages rekindled memories of folklore, 'wives'-tales' and old sayings, which I questioned at the time (as children do) from family, friends, and elderly neighbours. I can recall picking 'Aunt Burrell', the old lady who lived next door, a bunch of daisies, fern leaves, and dandelions. I wrapped them in a sheet of flowered paper and tied them with a yellow ribbon. When I gave them to her she shouted 'Piss-the-beds' and threw them in the bin in disgust! The following day, I saw her hanging out bed linen. Riddled with guilt, I ran and told my mother that 'Aunt Burrell' had wet the bed and it was all my fault because I gave her the flowers. My mother laughed and tried to convince me otherwise, but in my child's mind, I really believed that it was my fault. I didn't go near a dandelion for years, let alone pick one in fear that it might happen again. I later discovered that her hot water bottle had burst during the night. Deep down I never really forgave her for not telling me, as for the best part of five years I had been blaming myself for something that wasn't even my fault! Just one of many examples of how superstition can confuse the mind of an innocent child.

1 Baby Lore

In days of old it was very difficult to impose a Christian view upon ignorant village folk, especially the people who lived in the small remote villages where old folk and woodsmen kept the old traditional pagan stories alive of witches, were-wolves, vampires and other monstrous beasts. There was no need for a doctor, at least not in the remote villages. In the case of serious injuries, the 'bone-setter' would be sent for, who, no doubt, used comfrey which was well-known for its power to aid the speedy knitting together of fractured bone ends, hence the country name for comfrey: 'knit-bone'. It was also a good remedy for rheumatism, arthritis, and weak liga-ments. The liquid extracted from the root was used to treat all disorders of the chest.

The local blacksmith or the barber also served as the village dentist. A good stiff drink was all he had to offer his patient while he pulled out the bad tooth with a pair of pliers. If they could afford to buy them, folk would chew on a fresh clove to ease the pain of toothache. Then of course there was the midwife, and the 'wise-woman' whose magical potions (which sometimes worked effectively on sick villagers), probably consisted of herbs alone with a touch of magic thrown in for free!

In the early 1800s the average village had 14 births and 11 deaths yearly. All births took place in the home and were taken care of by the family, old women from the village or the local midwife. Many babies died before the age of two and often through simple lack of hygiene women died from childbed-fever, even after an uncomplicated birth. In the past extreme measures were taken to protect a woman throughout her pregnancy. Not only did she refrain from carrying out any household tasks but in some very primitive villages was forced to retire into a completely secluded place until after the birth of the child, as they believed that evil spirits surrounded a woman during pregnancy and her touch might contaminate others.

A child born with a birthmark (especially if it was on the face), was thought to be a child of the Devil. 'It bears the Devil's mark' the villagers would say. The cause of the birthmark was thought to be the result of the woman being touched by unseen spirits, or it was a sign that she had been unfaithful to her husband and the mark was an act of punishment. Many attempts were made to try to remove the mark, from beating the child daily with an elder branch to rubbing the mark with the fresh saliva from a virgin. If the midwife hadn't already killed the child to protect the family and the village itself from being cursed, the child would be wrapped in a sack, smuggled out of the house late at night and sold to the gypsies. The child, if a boy, would be sold for no more than one pound, but a girl would fetch as much as three pounds as she would be of more use to the gypsy.

The gypsy would travel from village to village to peddle his wares. If a customer should refuse to buy, the girl would be dragged out of the caravan and the hooded cape which she wore to cover her face would be removed. The people would turn their heads away in horror and would most definitely pay him immediately in fear of being cursed. However, those of less generosity needed a little persuasion.

The gypsy would probably have said something like this:

'Behold, look at the face which bears the mark of the Devil;
     She will curse your unborn children, and evil
Will sweep through your fields quicker than a swarm of locust.
     Look into the eyes of the Evil One if you dare,
Or have pity on a humble gypsy and buy my wares!'

Children born deaf, blind, or deformed in any way were thought to be evil. If the midwife had been merciful and spared the child, it led a life of poverty, cruelty, and humiliation, spending most of the daylight in hiding. For centuries children born with epilepsy were thought to be mad and possessed by demons. They were chained up in some old barn and kept out of sight while the priest was sent for whose job was to try to expel the demons from the supposedly

possessed. Although years ago most of the folk who lived in
the small villages were all God-fearing people they were still
very superstitious. The young expectant mother was told all
manner of things. If she walked over a newly-dug grave the
baby would be born dead. To spin during her pregnancy
would cause the child to die by strangling itself with the
umbilical cord: and if, whilst sewing, she should prick her
finger she would haemorrhage to death after the birth. Probably one of the oldest superstitions around at that time was
that if a hare should cross the path of a pregnant woman the
child would be born with a 'hare-lip'. (I expect this was
because witches were supposed to be able to change themselves into hares).

According to superstition if the mother should drape the
cradle before the birth, the child would not be born alive. It
was also considered unlucky to rock the cradle before the
child was born, and again to rock the cradle empty before the
child had been christened was tempting fate. Once the cradle
had been rocked with a child in it, then it was safe to rock it
empty when not in use.

> Rock a cradle empty,
> Babies you shall have a plenty.

It is also equally unlucky to rock an empty pram for the
same reason. An empty pram should never be brought into
the house. To do so would entice misfortune. The husband
should buy the pram a week before the birth. This is an old
custom which has been carried out in my family for years.
Before my sister was born my father bought a new pram but
kept it in his car and it wasn't allowed to stand empty in the
house until we had been informed of the birth.

One of my great-grandmother Louisa's old sayings was:

> If in your house an empty pram should lie,
> Empty it shall stay
> For the child will surely die.

After the birth of my new baby sister I became very
jealous (something I'm sure all families experience). I con-

stantly demanded more attention, and had a few temper tantrums, not to mention the odd smack! My pet guinea-pig, Squeaky didn't take too kindly to being dressed-up and bumped about all day in a doll's pram, so to solve the problem my mother brought me a life-size baby doll. Squeaky was happy back in her cage, and I was content with my new doll, which soon caused problems, one in particular which I shall never forget.

I was playing with my doll in the garden, keeping an eye on my sister, who was sleeping peacefully until Harry, next door's cat, suddenly jumped over the wall onto the hood of the pram and woke her up. My mother, hearing Helen screaming, came out and took her inside. I pushed Harry back over the wall, and seeing the pram empty I pinched some of the new baby clothes off the washing line, dressed my doll in them and put the doll into the pram covered with a blanket. A few hours later, our old friend and family doctor popped in to see my mother and the new arrival. Saying 'Hello' to me and patting me on the head, he peered into the pram. 'What a beautiful baby,' he said, rocking the pram gently, and making gurgling noises. I ran inside and told my mother. In fits of laughter, she came running out with my sister in her arms. We stood and watched him make a spectacle of himself until finally she shouted, 'Doctor Ball, why don't you come inside and see the real baby!' He turned around looking most confused. 'I thought the child looked rather pale. My word, I shall have to remember to bring my glasses with me next time,' he said. Not long after this episode he had a heart attack and died. He was a very well-respected man, loved by all who knew him and is sadly missed.

The day and time on which a child is born has always been of great importance but even how a child is delivered has its own significance and superstition as you will see:

A child that is delivered in a caul will be protected throughout his or her life. He will never drown or be destroyed by fire.
A child born by a Caesarian section will have the gift of second sight and possess unusual strength.
A 'footling-child' born by a breach birth is said to have

the power to heal, especially those suffering from arthritis and other muscular disorders.

If a child is delivered with the umbilical cord around its neck, the child, especially if a girl, will constantly be bound throughout life, not only to her family but to taking upon herself the worries and difficult tasks of others.

A child born at twilight will be conscious of the 'unseen'. A child born on the Eve of Hallowe'en (October 30th) will be able to see passing souls.

A child born on Good Friday will carry grief throughout his or her life, but will be given the gift of easing the sorrows of others.

The seventh child born of a seventh child (especially a boy), is born lucky, and will be successful in everything he undertakes, especially in love and business. These children are very talented and are by nature born leaders.

If a baby boy is born with a good head of hair and after the age of three a lock of hair be cut and kept, in later life he will never go bald. (This custom only applies to the first born son). A baby that is born with hairs on its arms and legs will grow to be rich. Dark hair on the back of the child's neck is a sure sign of temper and ruthlessness.

A baby born with very dark moles on its body is said to be very headstrong, bad-tempered but extremely clever. A baby that is born with a double crown, is indeed born very lucky. Good luck is said to descend upon the first person who carries the child outdoors for the first time after the mother has handled the child. The double crown is also called the 'sign of the crossing paths' which means the possessor will travel.

It is most unlucky for a child to be born with teeth, even if only one or two. It is considered very unlucky for a child, especially a boy, to be born on December 28th, as it was on this never-to-be-forgotten day that King Herod of Judea ordered the massacre of the children. Although looked upon as an ill-omen for a child to be born with an extra finger on each hand, in some parts of Africa it was considered to be most fortunate. The finger, which in many cases wasn't properly formed, would be bound tightly daily until the loose flesh eventually fell off.

In the past, any deformity of the lower limbs, particularly of both legs and feet, was considered to be the work of the Devil. The ill fortune of the afflicted child reflected bad luck upon the family. The mother was able to hide the child's disability and nurse him until he was able to walk and fend for himself. Then, through fear and ignorance from the other village folk, the child was kept outside of the house away from the other children in case any harm should befall them. No one would show the child any compassion in fear of being cursed by Satan, as in their eyes, through their act of kindness they were sinning against God.

According to an old superstition, if a child is born with a full moon on the seventh fingernail counting from the little finger from the left hand (the first finger on the right hand) it will be blessed with seven years of good fortune, but will suffer great sorrow for the rest of its life. If the child is a girl, after the seven years of good fortune, she can try to reverse her fate by calling upon the Moon Goddess Diana for help. If her quest is granted a hare will be sighted after the passing of seven full moons.

My grandmother was born with two small bumps on the right side of her head. When she was four years old she asked her mother what they were and she told her that they were 'bumps of knowledge'. For years I have been trying to persuade her to have her 'head read' purely out of interest. But as the old saying goes, 'You can lead a horse to water but you can't make it drink!'

Her mother, Louisa had an old saying:

> A child will never have reason to cover his head
> If a lock of hair be cut and kept.

Her first-born, Alfred, had the most beautiful blonde curly hair. She cut a single lock and kept it in a small box placed in front of his photograph which stood on top of the dresser beside her bed. Sadly, he was killed at a very young age during the first world war. After she had received the news of his death she put the lock of hair into a wooden chest where it remained until her death. The superstition of the 'cutting of the hair' is to prevent the child from hair loss in later life. This custom only applies to the first born son, and the hair must not be cut until the child is three years of age. Unfortunately, in my great uncle's case, he didn't live long enough to prove the superstition. After the birth of her sixth son, William, she was so convinced that he was going to die she sent for the vicar to christen him so that he could be buried in hallowed ground. With all the family present, he was christened in the kitchen beside the fire. As far as I know, there wasn't anything medically wrong with him. Throughout his childhood he was by no means a sickly child; and furthermore, he has just celebrated his eightieth birthday!

Her eighth child, Frederick, was not only born with a double crown, but with very unusual dark moles up his nostrils! This may sound absurd but it's true. Louisa was unaware that he had them because they weren't visible. A few years later, a gypsy knocked at her door selling charms, pegs, and lucky lace. On seeing her son, the gypsy bent down and lifted his head upwards, then tilted his head from side to side. 'Moles,' she muttered, 'unusual moles, I've never seen them as high up as this before in a young child. They're very lucky. The lad will travel far, and mix with folk in high places. He bears the mark of the "crossing paths" too – indeed a very fortunate child.' And with that she left. As he got older, one mole grew down and was quite visible on the inside of his left nostril. When he was in his late teens he had his palm read by a local fortune-teller. She told him that he was born with a double crown and that he would travel the world because the significance of the double crown is 'crossing paths' meaning that the possesser would travel and break bread in two countries, which he did. He travelled all over from Scotland to India. She didn't mention anything about his moles, but what the first gypsy predicted when he was a child did come true. During the second world war, whilst based in a small village in Italy he saw an apparition of a soldier dressed in full uniform ready for combat. Some time after the war, he and his wife appeared on the David Frost show. He was asked to relate his experience as the topic of the show was 'ghostly happenings.' She said that he would 'mix with folk in high places'. I believe that this is what she foresaw.

Being the mother of ten children herself, Louisa was often called upon to assist at births, and to help lay out the dead. She once helped to deliver a baby boy which was born with a caul over its face. Due to complications, the doctor had to be summoned. The birth was a difficult one, and left the mother very weak afterwards. She didn't want to part with the caul but she desperately needed the money to pay the doctor's bill. During the early hours of the morning, Louisa took the caul down to the docks where she sold it to a local fisherman for the sum of five pounds. When she returned she found the mother dead; the child was still cradled in her arms alive and healthy. On another occasion, she assisted at the birth of twin girls; both were born with the caul over the faces.

It is quite rare and very lucky for a child to be born in a caul, which is a soft thin layer of skin that covers part of the head and face almost like a veil. A child that is born in a caul will be protected against drowning and will never be harmed by fire. This is the true superstition of the caul. And mothers who were superstitious and aware of the legend would by no means part with it. If a 'caul birth' child died at a young age they were sometimes buried with the caul. As it was looked upon as a safeguard against fire, this act was probably undertaken to ensure that the child's soul would go to Heaven. It was also believed that the child would be immune against all disease, protected against any form of evil, and able to read the thoughts of others. In the past, children that were born in cauls were paid to heal the sick and dying, as they were thought to have special healing powers. They were also said to be able to revive the dead, especially if death was by drowning. In the late 17th century cauls were sold to seafaring people for as much as thirty-five pounds. Once the caul was on board the ship, they believed that it would protect everyone from drowning, keep storms at bay, and prevent shipwreck. Still today, cauls are sold as charms to sailors and fishermen, especially in the small remote fishing villages of Devon and Cornwall.

A man (whose identity I shall reveal later) was born in a caul, but whether the caul was sold or kept is beyond my knowledge. Throughout his life he has come close to death seven times, each time either by fire or water. He survived without any serious injuries. He was born on October 13th 1919, which, as you will see later, is very significant. The legend connected with the caul (that a child will never drown or be destroyed by fire), in this man's case appears to be fact rather than superstition. There is no plausible explanation that can account for the luck, and I use that word lightly, that this man has had. I can say without any doubt that I truly believe that he was protected throughout his life, as I personally do not believe in sheer luck, fate, or coincidence. After reading his story, you can judge for yourself.

When war broke out, he joined the Mercantile Marine, which was later re-named the Merchant Navy. His ship was on passage to Calais from Harwich. At the time, they were unaware that it was the first day that Hitler had sown magnetic mines in the North Sea. Miraculously the ship avoided them. On sighting three ships which were sinking, they launched a thirty-foot long lifeboat and were able to row out and rescue some of the people who were covered in fuel-oil and in danger of drowning. He saw a bundle floating towards him, and on reaching it he found that it was a baby, covered in oil, screaming lustily. He returned to his ship with the child still in his care. Later, the survivors were taken to the local hospital, and the child (a boy less than a year old) was reunited with its mother who had also been saved from the sea that claimed many lives that night. At the time of Dunkirk he was rescuing allied soldiers from the beaches. Soon after Dunkirk, and the evacuation of the Channel Islands (just before the Germans invaded), on arriving back to England his ship was shelled by his own Navy due to all the confusion at the time.

In October 1940 he left the Merchant Navy and joined the Royal Navy. He was drafted to an old paddle-steamer build in 1906, which was serving as a mine-sweeper in the North Sea. One evening, whilst posted at Harwich he was returning to his ship during an air raid. He took shelter in a shop doorway. On hearing some bombs falling, he ran further up the street and laid down flat in a gutter. Just seconds later, a bomb completely destroyed the shop where he had been standing. Two people in the flat above the shop were instantly killed.

Three weeks later his ship was sunk by a German bomber. The bomb went straight through his cabin instantly killing his two shipmates, asleep in their bunks. Minutes before it happened, he changed watch with another shipmate. If he hadn't volunteered to keep watch he would still have been asleep in the cabin when the bomb had hit.

His next ship was engaged in commando raids and landing troups on beachheads during invasions. 'We survivied a bomb that went right through the ship on the Dieppe raid. We did landings in North Africa, Sicily, and Italy. But the most terrifying of all, with many ships sunk and a huge loss of lives took place at Salerno. We were dive-bombed by Stukas for twenty-four hours; how we survived was a miracle. We came back to England. In the early hours of "D" Day we landed the 47th Royal Marine Commandos at Arromanche in France. In spite of all this we only lost two of our crew.'

Before I go any further I would like to state the following: I haven't in any way altered or 'spiced-up' this account in order to make it more intriguing to read. If any event doesn't correspond with a given date I hold no responsibility. I have presented the facts as they were given to me and to my knowledge they are correct. For personal reasons, I purposely excluded the many sordid details, horrors, and events which took place during the war and coincided with this story.

After the war disaster struck again, endangering not only his own life but his family's as well. On January 31st 1953 the East coast of England was flooded by the North Sea. His family had to be rescued by the fire brigade in a small rowing boat from one of the upstairs bedroom windows. By this time the entire house was flooded, including the bedrooms. Six people drowned that night in Harwich.

Not long after the flood he was taken ill with a duodenal ulcer. He was rushed into hospital where his wife was told that he had only hours to live. He left the hospital a few weeks later.

Then on January 13th 1979 there was a gas explosion in the house next door to his while the occupants were away on holiday. At the time of the explosion, (2.00 a.m.) he and his wife were asleep in bed. They awakened, and to their horror the house had been completely destroyed, a fire had started and rubble surrounded them. Luckily, with assistance, they managed to crawl downstairs to safety, and the only injury was a cut on his wife's hand.

Afterwards when I asked him if he believed in the superstition he told me modestly. 'I'm not at all superstitious, but I suppose one could say that the many things that have happened to me throughout my life indicate that I've been lucky. He paused and laughed before adding: 'I do know that I was born with a double crown which is supposed to be very lucky!'

13 Unlucky For Some: The number thirteen has always been associated with superstition and bad luck, but it isn't as grossly unlucky as people tend to think. Without consulting my diary, I can think of five people whose birthday falls on the thirteenth, (two of whom are family). All five were born on October 13th, but three were actually born on Friday the thirteenth. The stigma connected with the number thirteen didn't apply to these people, in fact it was the complete reverse. Apart from sharing the same birth date they have two other things in common: they all wear glasses, and not one of them is in the least superstitious! Personally, I would say that it's a 'chancy' number, and for the sake of superstition I tend to play-safe to avoid tempting the hands of fate. There are literally hundreds of rituals that are carried out (especially when Friday does happen to fall on the thirteenth) to prevent anything disastrous or out of the ordinary from happening. As a rule, I never discuss future events connected with money, and I wouldn't even contemplate sending or giving a close friend a gift made of glass.

Why are some people luckier than others? Why do some people sail through the whole of their lives quite easily when others are faced with a continuous battle? Why are some people always in the right place at the right time? Even when they do find themselves in the wrong place at the wrong time they still seem to come up smelling of roses! Some people who believe in the Christian teachings are convinced that a guardian angel keeps a watchful eye over them, or the hand of God plays a great part in the fate of their lives. Others consult the stars, palmistry, or revert to the ancient art of tea-leaf reading. Through my own personal experiences, I believe that everything happens for a reason and is usually of significance or has a hidden meaning. Luck, fate, or coincidence has nothing to do with it. A prime example is the man whose story I have already related to you, and for a person who regards superstition as old 'mumbo-jumbo', he's certainly had far more than his fair share of lucky escapes. In fact, after reading his story my first reaction was: 'This man's a jinx! The type of person that chaos follows like a bad smell and strikes wherever he goes!' But being the person that I am, after studying and reading his account over and over again, the answer, or the 'plausible explanation' that I had been looking for had been staring right at me all the time. All the dates of the events which took place once calculated added up to thirteen, as did his date of birth, and even his name!

Numbers in General

The basic rules of numerology are fairly straightforward and once grasped it can be used for business affairs, future events (such as planning in advance what would be the best time of the year to book your holiday). Or you could use it for personal use to find out your lucky numbers, days of the week, month of the year, and so on. This ancient method has been used for centuries, and no doubt will be used for centuries to come. It is quick, simple, and it works! And the good news is, you don't have to be a mathematical genius to work it out, as this system consists of addition only!

All numbers are singular and fall in between a scale consisting of the numbers one to nine. A double digit number is reduced to a singular by adding the two numbers together. So 17 becomes $1 + 7 = 8$. In addition to this 97 becomes 7. ($9 + 7 = 16 = 1 + 6 = 7$). Any number ending in a 0, e.g. 10, 50, 100, is changed from a double digit number to a singular and takes the luck of the first number. So 10 becomes 1; 50 becomes 5 and 100 becomes 1. On calculation other numbers may be added if of significance such as a birth date, lucky number, or a number that signifies the day, month, or year of calculation.

Numbers of the Alphabet

1	2	3	4	5	6	7	8	9
A	B	C	D	E	F	G	H	I
J	K	L	M	N	O	P	Q	R
S	T	U	V	W	X	Y	Z	

Days of the Week

SUNDAY	–1	THURSDAY	–5
MONDAY	–2	FRIDAY	–6
TUESDAY	–3	SATURDAY	–7
WEDNESDAY	–4		

Numbers from Ten to Twenty

10 = 1 (1 + 0 = 1)
11 = 2 (1 + 1 = 2)
12 = 3 (1 + 2 = 3)
13 = 4 (1 + 3 = 4)
14 = 5 (1 + 4 = 5)
15 = 6 (1 + 5 = 6)
16 = 7 (1 + 6 = 7)
17 = 8 (1 + 7 = 8)
18 = 9 (1 + 8 = 9)
19 = 1 (1 + 9 = 10 = 1 + 0 = 1)
20 = 2 (2 + 0 = 2)

Months of the Year

JANUARY – 1
FEBRUARY – 2
MARCH – 3
APRIL – 4
MAY – 5
JUNE – 6
JULY – 7
AUGUST – 8
SEPTEMBER – 9
OCTOBER – 1 (10 = 1 + 0 = 1)
NOVEMBER – 2 (11 = 1 + 1 = 2)
DECEMBER – 3 (12 = 1 + 2 = 3)

To Calculate your Name

Suppose your name is Helen Price. To find your own personal lucky number calculate your name using the alphabet system as follows:

H E L E N P R I C E

8+ 5+ 3+ 5+ 5+ 7+ 9+ 9+ 3+ 5 = 59 = 5 + 9 = 14 = 1 + 4 = 5

So from calculating her name, we arrived at the number 5 which is her personal lucky number. Any of its multiples, i.e. 25, 35, 45, etc, and of course 50 will also prove to be lucky. The number 14 could also serve her well as 1 + 4 = 5. The number five also marks her three lucky letters: E, N, W. This method works particularly well in the interest of business as the number five also indicates that Thursday (being the fifth day of the week), and May (being the fifth month of the year), are to her advantage, especially when important decisions have to be made concerning current issues, investments, and future events.

Some will argue that your date of birth once calculated is your true lucky number, but as already mentioned, you can use the two systems either together or separately; one for business affairs, and the other for personal use only. I have found that it's a matter of 'knowing' which system is right for a specific purpose rather than abiding by the rules. Once you have found a system that works well for you it is wise not to change from the first remaining single number (if it is serving you well), whether you arrived at that number by calculating your name, date of birth, or even your credit card number!

To Calculate your Date of Birth

Example: JULY 23rd 1986 = (JULY = 7/23 = 2 + 3 = 5/19 = 1/ 86 = 8 + 6 = 14 = 1 + 4 = 5) So July 23rd 1986 = 7 + 5 + 1 + 5 = 18 = (1 + 8 = 9)

So suppose that you were born on September 25th 1962, you would calculate as the following: 9 + 7 + 1 + 8 = 25 = (2 + 5 = 7). Other numbers may be added to the last digit such as the number of your birth sign, name, age, etc.

Ronald William Chilver (whose story I have related) once calculated left two remaining numbers thirteen and four, as did his date of birth after his personal lucky number being four (as derived from his name) had been added to the last digit. The dates of the events which took place also left the two same remaining numbers as you will see. I have added certain numbers of significance to some of the dates which were not carefully selected in order to arrive at the given numbers thirteen and four after calculation.

His Name Once Calculated: 103 = 1 + 0 + 3 = 13 = (1 + 3 = 4)

Date of Birth & Lucky Number:

MONDAY 13th OCTOBER 1919:

BECOMES

2 + 4 + 1 + 1 + 1 + 4 = 13 = (1 + 3 = 4)

NOVEMBER 19th 1939: 2 + 1 + 1 + 3 = 7 + 6 = 13 = (1 + 3 = 4)

I have added a six to the last digit because I made the calculation on the sixth day of the sixth month.

JANUARY 31st 1953: $1 + 4 + 1 + 8 = 14 = 1 + 4 = 5 + 8 = 13 = (1 + 3 = 4)$

At the time of the flood he lived at number 44 which is lucky within itself as 44 is a multiple of 4. On the same principle 8 is also a multiple of 4 which is the reason why I have added the number eight to the last single digit.

JANUARY 13th 1979: $1 + 4 + 1 + 7 = 13 = (1 + 3 = 4)$

(JAN $= 1/13 = 4$, $(1 + 3)/19 = 1$, $(1 + 9 = 10 = 1)/79 = 7$, $(7 + 9 = 16 = 7)$

As you can see the above date clearly adds up to thirteen, and from the number thirteen we arrive back at the number four which is valid, being derived from his name. At the time of the explosion he lived at number 24, which again is in his favour as 24 is also a multiple of 4, $(6 \times 4 = 24)$. The number twenty-four is very significant. When reduced to a singular number and then added to the number of the day on which January 13th 1979 fell, it also added up to a straight thirteen as you will see, and from this we arrive back to the number four, the same two remaining numbers as did his name, date of birth, and all the given dates after calculation.

The above date fell on a Saturday, thus Saturday = 7 (being the seventh day of the week). The number $24 = (2 + 4 = 6)$. So $6 + 7 = 13 = (1 + 3 = 4)$.

There is no doubt in mind that he is still alive today because he was protected throughout his life, and unbeknown to him, the numbers thirteen and four were vastly important and played a major part in controlling his destiny. Even when in a situation where his life was endangered he was spared, and so were the lives of loved ones who were with him at the time. They were always protected through him. I believe that everybody has someone watching over them to guide their every move in times of trouble. Even though I strongly adhere to superstition and happenings that cannot be accounted for, I also believe that there is one supreme power above all, which marks out our lives before we are even conceived. And as it is written, so it shall be done!

An old traditional custom which is still very much alive today is that of a woman going to be 'churched'. After the birth of a new born baby the first steps that a mother should take outside the house should be to church to thank God for a safe pregnancy, delivery, and a healthy baby. The child was left at home either in the care of the father or the grandparents, as for the father to attend was considered to be unlucky and would most certainly entice misfortune. Furthermore, to ignore totally this religious act was looked upon as a bad omen for the mother as well as the child. This custom in particular, I have found, is often disregarded, especially by young single, non-religious mothers. I can think of eight friends who all had reason to rejoice and praise God after giving birth to perfectly formed, beautiful healthy babies, but ignored this ritual, mainly because through ignorance they were unaware of the custom. It saddens me to think that what was once respected and valued is no longer considered to be important in this modern day world in which we live. This custom is one which my grandmother can recall well. Coming from a large family and being the eldest girl, she has seen this tradition carried out many times by her mother. My grandmother recalls: 'As soon as my mother was well enough, after resting in bed for 12 to 14 days after giving birth, she would put on her white silk headscarf, which she only wore on special occasions. She'd take with her a candle made from pure beeswax, and a fresh homemade cake as a gift for the Vicar's wife. Father would be out back chopping wood, but no words ever passed between them. Before she reached the gate you could bet your last penny that the young 'un would be screaming, but she would never look back, to do so was unlucky.' Even though her mother conceived thirteen times, only six of her children (that were born alive) survived to adulthood, which was why the tradition was so very important then, simply because many babies were either stillborn, or weak, and died at a young age, and many mothers died during childbirth.

I never knew that my own mother was churched after having me until I began researching for this book.

It is an old tradition in London, especially amongst the Costermongers (market traders and barrow people) to give money to a newly born baby when passed by the mother and the child. A silver coin would be put into the baby's hand if awake. If the child was sleeping peacefully in the pram then the coin was placed underneath the baby's pillow. A newly born baby would not normally have a pillow, for obvious reasons, it was used purposely to slide the coins underneath the baby's head. The pillow was also a sign to let people know that it was the child's first day outside the house. My mother recalls: 'When I came out of hospital, Betty gave me a soft, white, beautifully embroidered pillow, and told me to put it in your pram when I took you outside for the first time. I had to take you to your grandparents' house first before I could go to be churched. I walked, with you in the pram, all the way down the market, and by the time I had reached the end of the road I had collected over six pounds in coins which was a fair amount of money then. As you were asleep, all the coins were placed underneath the pillow, and on seeing this, your grandfather woke you up, and put a coin in your hand.' (I expect that he did this because it is traditional for the father or the grandfather to put the first coin into the child's hand). This London tradition is the equivalent to the old country superstition: it is unlucky to pass a newborn child unless a gift is given.

The following service is taken from the original Book of Common Prayer which was compiled in 1547 and first published in 1662.

The Thanksgiving Of A Woman After Child-Birth.
Commonly Called
'The Churching Of A Woman.'

The woman, at the usual time after her delivery, shall come into the church decently apparelled, and there shall kneel down in some convenient place, and hath been accustomed, or as the ordinary shall direct. And then the Priest shall say unto her:

'Forasmuch as it hath pleased Almighty God of his goodness to give you safe deliverance, and hath preserved you in great danger of child-birth; you shall therefore give hearty thanks unto God, and say:

PSALM CXXVII NISI DOMINUS

Except the Lord build the house; their labour is lost that build it.

Except the Lord keep the City; the watchman waketh but in vain.

It is but lost labour that ye haste to rise up early, and so late take rest, and eat the bread of carefulness: For so he giveth his beloved sheep.

Lo, children and the fruit of the womb; are an heritage and gift that cometh of the Lord.

Like as the arrows in the hand of the giant; even so are the young children.

Happy is the man that hath his quiver full of them; they shall not be ashamed when they speak with their enemies in the gate.

Glory be to the Father, and to the Son, and to the Holy Ghost.

As it was in the beginning, is now, and ever shall be, World Without End. Amen.

> *Then the Priest shall say,*
> Let us pray.
> Lord, have mercy upon us.
> Christ, have mercy upon us.
> Lord, have mercy upon us.

Our Father, which art in Heaven, Hallowed be thy Name; Thy Kingdom come. Thy will be done in earth, As it is in Heaven. Give us this day our daily bread, And forgive us our trespasses, as we forgive them that trespass against us: And lead us not into temptation; But deliver us from evil: For thine is the Kingdom, the power, and the glory, For ever, and ever. Amen.

Minister: O Lord, save this woman thy servant.
Answer: Who putteth her trust in thee.
Minister: Be thou to her a strong tower;
Answer: From the face of her enemy.
Minister: Lord, hear our prayer,
Answer: And let our cry come unto thee.
Minister: Let us pray.

O Almighty God, we give thee humble thanks for that thou hast vouchsafed to deliver this woman thy servant from the great pain and peril of Child-Birth; grant, we beseech thee, most merciful Father, that she, through thy help, may both faithfully live, and walk according to thy will, in this present life: And also may be partaker of everlasting glory in the life to come; Through Jesus Christ our Lord. Amen.

The woman that cometh to give her thanks, must offer accustomed offerings; And, if there be a communion, it is convenient that she receive the Holy Communion.

(Extracts from the *Book of Common Prayer* of 1662, the rights which are vested in the Crown in perpetuity within the United Kingdom, are reproduced by permission of the Crown's Patentee, Cambridge University Press.)

Again, even after the birth, mothers were advised against doing certain things in case any harm should befall the child, as it was believed that in between birth and baptism the innocent child was in great danger from the Evil powers of Satan.

My grandmother was advised by her mother always to wear a silver thimble when going to the water pump the first time after having a new baby (it was considered extremely unlucky for the mother and the child if she didn't); never to rinse the nappies in cold water, or to wash the hands in cold water if 'unwell', and especially not whilst breastfeeding! And finally: should a nursing mother stand in a cold kitchen for too long, it would turn her milk sour!

To weigh a child before it was a year old was unheard of; and to step over a crawling child would stunt its growth for sure! It just goes to show how superstitions change, and become somewhat distorted through the passing years for the sake of human convenience. As my mother used to tell me at a young age smoking would stunt my growth. But it didn't deter me from taking up the disgusting habit!

My other grandmother was also advised not to rinse the nappies in cold water, or to immerse the hands in cold water shortly after the birth of a new baby. (I don't know the significance of this superstition as my grandmothers never questioned the reason why, they merely did what was asked of them out of respect). She was also told always to keep a child's first 'milk' tooth; never to cut a baby's nails but to bite them until the child was a year old; and that 'A baby has only got the warmth that you give it.' By this, she meant body warmth, not love. As they didn't have central heating in the past, it was necessary to make sure that the infant was kept nice and warm throughout the night whilst sleeping. The baby would be tightly wrapped in a shawl with its hands tucked inside. This prevented the child from throwing off the over blankets and scratching its face. The baby was always laid on its side facing the mother's bed, so that the mother could see the child's face from her bedside at all times. This also prevented the child from choking should he vomit.

> 'Let a lying child cry
> To fend off the Evil Eye.'

One of my great-grandmother's old familiar sayings, although not one that many mothers would agree with, as there is nothing worse than a screaming infant!

According to old folklore a newly born child (especially if unbaptized), was in great danger from all evil, including fairies, until it had sneezed, then it was thought to be safe to enter into the world of 'living men'.

Have you ever wondered why people say 'God bless you' when you sneeze? The reason for this primitive saying is very simple, and is still frequently used by many today. The fact that the saying 'God bless you' can only be used after someone else has actually sneezed is very significant. On sneezing, the heart misses a beat, and during that split second (especially in the case of a newly born child), it was believed that the 'Devil' could enter the child's body through the mouth and possess the child's innocent soul. Therefore, once the child had sneezed, the words 'God bless you' were said to ward off the Devil, and the child was thought to be safe from any further enchantment.

In old folklore literally everything has a meaning or is of some significance, as you will see by the following superstitions.

Fingers: Long slim fingers belong to those of talent. Short fat fingers belong to persons with an open mind and loving nature. A short fat thumb signifies a shrewd mind; a long slim thumb is a sure sign of temper! Never trust a man who has a crooked 'baby' finger; money is his one and only passion, and he will do everything within his power to obtain it, but the 'itch' will soon set in motion once the money is in his hand. Such people are compulsive, unable to save or spend money wisely. An old legend declares that if the third finger is longer than the middle finger, the owner is a Werewolf! (I find this superstition hard to believe but nevertheless, beware, you have been forewarned).

Hands: If a child laughs and kicks with its hands open wide, palms relaxed and the fingers evenly outstretched, he will grow up to be extremely kind, loving, and generous. (The same applies if the child is a girl). If the fists are kept tightly clenched, the child will grow up to be mean, bad tempered, and 'tight-fisted' (especially where money is concerned). Deep red lines on the palms of the hands represent strength and courage; whilst pale thin lines are a sign of weakness and poor health. Wide hands belong to ambitious, strong-willed persons, and tend to be very critical, of themselves as well as others. Narrow hands belong to those of a quiet, rather shy, and loving nature.

Nails: Never cut a child's nails until it is a year old; if you do, it may grow up to be 'light-fingered!' The mother should bite them herself during the first twelve months. My mother bit my nails until I was a year old, as did her mother, and her mother before her; throughout life our nails have always grown profusely. My younger and only sister didn't have her nails bitten and she is forever complaining, as her nails are very weak and hardly ever grow at all! You can tell by looking at the nails if a person has a certain illness or disease. Ridges on the nails are a sure sign of poor health. When spots are found on several nails, it is a sign of the nervous system. When spots are due to injury, in time, as the nail grows, the spot will grow out. Very brittle nails are said to be a sign of gout. I have found the above to be true. Since my illness I have developed deep ridges and spots on my nails, and they are now very brittle. My condition is of the nervous system, which accounts for the ridges and spots; and the brittle nails are the result of Erythromelalgia – an inflammatory disease which has been associated with gout in the past, due to extreme constant heat and swelling of the legs and feet.

Naturally yellowish nails are stronger than milky white ones. It is also said that the moons on the nails will turn blue as the owner approaches death. When death is imminent, they will become black. The growth of the nails varies in different individuals. On young hands the growth is more rapid. Nails grow quicker in the summer than they do in the winter. The nails on the right hand grow faster than those on the left, and the nail on the second finger away from the thumb will grow quicker and stronger than any other nails: strange, but true. Do you ever stop to think what day it is when you cut your nails? This is a very old poem, that my grandmother can remember her aunt saying:

Cutting the Nails

Cut them on Monday, cut them for news,
Cut them on Tuesday, for a new pair of shoes,
Cut them on Wednesday, cut for a letter,
Cut them on Thursday, for something better,
Cut them on Friday, cut them for sorrow,
Cut them on Saturday, to see your sweetheart tomorrow,
Cut them on Sunday, your safety go seek,
For Satan will have you for the rest of the week!

Teeth: In some parts of the country, mothers used to tie a piece of rowan wood around the child's neck so that the fairies would have no power over the child to change it for one of their own weakly little offspring. The wood (especially when worn around the neck) was looked upon as a charm to protect the infant from any evil; it was also believed to prevent the child from pain when teething. The teething pegs which can be brought today probably originated from the ancient idea of using the rowan wood hung around the neck to chew on.

If the first tooth appears in the upper jaw, the child will be protected against serious illness throughout life. If the first tooth appears in the lower jaw the child will suffer great pain throughout life, but will induce love and happiness to all those worthy enough to accept this gift. If a child's teeth appear early, there will be another new arrival born into the family fairly soon!

Although never appreciated, a gap in between the top front teeth signifies wealth; whereas a gap in between the bottom teeth is considered unlucky. The owner will die poor but happy. Small, square, close-together teeth signify strength and good health. Long, narrow teeth are a promise of old age. A necklace made of human teeth (when worn by a man) will strengthen the body, soul, and the mind. When worn by a woman, it is said to arouse certain sexual desires!

Wisdom teeth (once extracted) should be kept, as they are very lucky; the teeth should be strung on a gold chain and worn close to the body, either on the arm as a bracelet, or around the neck close to the heart. If worn as earrings, again, thread the teeth through a hoop made of gold, never silver. Wisdom teeth bring luck to the owner, promising eternal life in the hereafter if buried with the deceased. When worn around the neck, they will ward off early senility.

Having just had all four wisdom teeth extracted, feeling sore and swollen, looking at them standing beside my typewriter in a glass bottle, uncanny as it may sound, I feel a close 'bond' towards them, rather like a mother does towards her child. But by no means am I comparing the pains and peril of childbirth to having wisdom teeth extracted, I'm merely using it as an example. For months (twelve to be exact) I endured pain, nausea, not to mention the endless sleepless nights; I constantly nurtured them with careful cleaning, brushing and regular salt rinses to keep them free from bacteria and infection. In the end, the pain, black eyes, swelling and headaches were soon over with and forgotten (well almost). Afterwards, a mother would naturally be delighted and overjoyed when handed her newborn baby, whereas I was presented with a bottle containing four of the most grotesque teeth that I had ever seen! I was disappointed to say the least.

As I intended to have them strung on to a gold necklace (and still do, when I can afford to), I wanted to make sure that they were extracted whole, and given to me afterwards. I was surprised by the dentist's reaction when I asked him this. I was afraid that he would think my request somewhat strange; but as it happened, he shared my belief, and told me that he had his own wisdom teeth strung onto a gold chain. He promised me that he would try his utmost to 'yank' them out whole, and deliver them to me the same day, which he did. When the day comes, I shall wear my teeth with pride; but for the meantime they are standing in a bottle, preserved in salt beside my typewriter.

My headmistress had her own remedy for preserving teeth which she related to me one summer during a school dental check-up. I was an inquisitive child, and very outspoken, which is why I can recall this incident so well. I was standing in line with the rest of the class waiting my turn. I couldn't understand why the headmistress didn't have the same teeth as my grandparents had: false teeth, or 'removable' teeth, I used to call them because my grandad never used to wear his top set, they were always left around the house in a glass of water, and moved around more times than he had had hot dinners! Everyone old whom I knew had the same teeth as my gran, so I just couldn't understand why she didn't. I made up my mind that I would go and ask her why she didn't have false teeth after I had seen the dentist. Instead of going back to the classroom afterwards, I walked over, and tugged at her skirt to get her attention. She quickly spun round on one heel, bent down, and glared at me; her small square glasses sat halfway down her nose, her murky green eyes fixed their gaze on to mine. I knew that look, I had known it well ever since I had called her an old bat! I didn't mean to, it just slipped out one day, besides, how was I to know that the new girl (who heard me and told her) was her grand-daughter! She kept me in every dinner-time for a week. Favouritism my gran said, she called her an old bat too, amongst other things. I was waiting for her to march me off to her office with my hands on my head, or even worse, a quick sharp smack on the backs of my legs (which she was renowned for doing when angry) and as I had interrupted her talking to the dentist's assistant, that's what I was expecting. 'What do you want?' she snapped.

'I want to ask you a question, Miss.'

'Well, hurry up, and then return to your class.'

'Why don't you wear false teeth like my gran does?'

'Selena, you are rude and disobedient, but as you are probably the only child who has enough nerve to ask me such a question, I will tell you. I brush my teeth twice a day with brandy, and have done for years, and I always rub a little into the gums last thing at night.'

'But I thought brandy was for drinking, Miss.'

'It is, but it's an excellent preserver, and so much nicer than toothpaste!'

As she walked me back to class we talked endlessly; I saw another side to her and I was going to apologize for calling her an old bat; but I soon changed my mind. As soon as we reached the classroom, she pushed me through the door, and shouted out loud (so that everyone could hear), 'Now take your seat, sit still and pay attention, you might learn something and thank me for it one day!' I did as I was told, got out my books and faced the front. I glanced over towards the door, she looked through the glass panel and smiled at me; she stood there for a few seconds and then walked away. That day I learned that teachers were human and have their off-days like everyone does, and that not all of them were (in a manner of speaking) old bats!

Long ago, village life was dominated by the church and still is today. Everyone was expected to attend mass on a Sunday, morning and evening. Everyone rich or poor gave generously. Noblemen tithed, and the peasantry were expected to put a penny in the communion plate at least! Dutiful wives were always more than willing to bake cakes, bread, and apple pies to be sold at fetes and garden fairs to help raise money for the church fund. The church provided help for the poor and needy, shelter for weary travellers, but most important of all, education. Many children were illiterate; their time would be spent working alongside their parents on the farm, and education, especially for girls, was considered an utter waste of time.

However, in *Badgeworth, A Church And Its Village*, by Christine Chambers, the first reference to a school occurs in 1704 when the Rev W. Stansby, a former Rector of Badgeworth, left certain lands in the Parish, the proceeds of the same to be devoted to the apprenticing 'of one or more children of honest day labourers' of Badgeworth, Churchdown, Cheltenham and other parishes, on condition that 'the children of Usurers, Beersellers, or persons of wicked life or conversation, either known or reputed as such, nor to any of the family of fallings of Badgeworth, except those remarkable for goodness or honesty.'

The school was merely an old cottage adjoining the church-yard, which remained as such until the late 1800s. Sadly, it is no longer in existence. A man named Thomas Bullock was paid three shillings a week to teach sixteen children to read and write, four children from each hamlet.

Thomas Bullock was parish clerk and the father of triplets, all of whom survived to manhood. The story of the birth of these triplets has been handed down through generations:

> Thomas was churning butter at a farmhouse, which is now Badgeworth Manor, when the midwife came to him and said: 'Thomas, your wife has brought you a nice little boy.' 'Oh, well and good,' said Thomas. Presently she came again: 'Thomas, your wife has brought you another boy.' 'The deuce she has,' said Thomas, but still kept on churning. Once again came the nurse. 'Thomas she've brought ye another boy.' 'Oh, dang it all,' said Thomas, 'I'll go and put a stop to this.' Then Thomas left churning and the arrivals stopped!

Before Thomas Bullock was put in charge of the education of Badgeworth, children of farmers used to go to the curate of Badgeworth, the Rev John Snap for instructions. This curate had a very bad reputation for cruelty and it is said that as punishment he would hang boys by their thumbs from the bacon-rack with their toes just touching the floor. This same curate was unpopular for another reason. Joseph Sadler was the churchwarden and John Snap used to hand down to him, after the service, a note saying: 'I, John Snap, curate, require the farmers of this parish to fetch me some coals.'

It is an old deep-rooted belief that a child does not thrive until it has been christened.

An old gypsy belief is that all children are sick and have no soul until they have been christened, then the illness will leave the child and its soul shall return pure from Heaven.

Before a child was christened, great lengths were taken in
order to protect the innocent child from the 'Evil Eye.' Charms
such as salt, sand, and silver coins were given purposely to
prevent the powers of evil from harming the child in any way.
Coral has always been very highly regarded as a charm to
ward off any source of evil. The coral beads were usually
hung around the child's neck in order to protect the newly-
born from the Devil's Eye. The Romans gave their children
red coral to wear to keep them safe from danger. Still today,
some Italians give, and wear red coral for protection and to
ward off the Evil Eye. The colour of the coral was also
important; the more vivid the red, the stronger its potency
was believed to be. It is also a renowned remedy for women
suffering from sterility. Legend has it that Medusa, the Gorgon
whose head turned beholders into stone, was severed and
then stolen by sea-nymphs, and the drops of blood sowed the
seeds of the red coral. By 'lore' and out of respect, coral should
always be worn traditionally in its natural form as twigs, or
stems, never as a 'fashioned' necklace of carefully cut shaped
beads.

Hyssop was also used as a charm. Hyssop is the 'Holy
Herb' because it was used for cleaning sacred places. It is also
mentioned in the scriptures: 'Purge me with hyssop and I
shall be clean' (Psalm 51 Verse 7). When Jesus was on the
cross, one disciple filled a sponge with vinegar and 'put it
upon hyssop and put it to his mouth. When Jesus therefore
had received the vinegar he said; "It is finished" and he
bowed his head and gave up the ghost' (John 19 v29–30).
Mothers would make a necklace from the herb and hang it
around the child's neck to ward off evil. The herb necklace
also signified purity.

Fennel, being just one of many anti-witch herbs, was em-
ployed together with St John's Wort as a preventative against
witchcraft, being hung over the baby's cradle.

In other parts of the country, mothers draped the cradle
with lavender and heather as a protection against any passing
souls and spirits.

Rosemary was used as a charm to ward off witchcraft and
to keep playful spirits at bay. Gypsies, above all, are great
lovers of this sweetly scented herb rosemary, also known as

the 'Queen of Hungary' worldwide. Gypsies hang rosemary sprigs around the windows and doors of their caravans as a protection against witches, and always put a fresh rosemary sprig under their children's beds, to prevent them from having nightmares.

An unchristened child was thought to suffer from far more illnesses than a child that had been christened. It was also believed that should a child die unchristened, it wasn't considered worthy enough to be buried in hallowed ground, and its soul would not be permitted to enter through the golden gates of Heaven, even though it is written in the scriptures: 'Suffer the little children to come unto me.' Instead, according to legend, the child's soul would be claimed by one of the seven Hounds of Hell, doomed to roam the hills and vales of the countryside for all eternity.

An old custom to wash away any lurking evil spirits is to spit on to the baby's head, then wash the child with virgin honey (clear honey), before it is christened. The purity of a virgin's kiss was said to be able to drive away any evil and had the power to protect the child from the Devil until it had been christened.

Let the woman who carries the child to the church also carry with her a piece of bread and cheese. This must be given to the first person she meets in the child's name. If the gift is accepted then all is well. (It is a great omen if the person is a poor tramp and eats the food at once). But if the gift is refused the stranger is wishing bad luck upon the unbaptized child. (An old Suffolk country custom.)

When taking the child to the church to be christened, the grandmother, who traditionally should carry the child until she reaches the church steps, should turn back once she has left the house and return inside with the child still in her arms, and leave on the table either her apron or scarf for good luck. (This is an old gypsy custom.)

In the 18th century, children were sometimes christened wearing a veil, which was worn underneath the traditional christening shawl or robe. Once a child had been christened wearing the veil it was considered most unlucky to completely remove it until six months had passed.

A child christened on the same day of the week as that on

which it was born will carry good luck and fortune throughout all his or her life. It is unlucky for a red-headed man or a
bald-headed man to be present at a christening, especially if
they are not direct family.

Most babies cry lustfully when being christened. Although
rather embarrassing for the parents, it is said to be extremely
lucky! A child that cries loudly throughout the whole service
will be a good strong sturdy fighter against the dark powers
of evil. (It isn't necessarily unlucky if a baby does not cry at
its own christening.)

Gifts Given

To give silver to a newly-christened child is a very old
traditional custom which is still carried out today.

Long ago, a newly-christened child would either have been
given a silver coin, a small box of some kind, or an apostle
spoon. Today the most popular gifts given are silver money
boxes, picture frames, engraved christening bangles (bearing
the child's name) or an engraved silver spoon. The christening spoons that are given today are the modern descendants
of apostle spoons. They were so called because each spoon
had a figure of one of the twelve apostles on the handle. The
spoons were made from gilt, and a broad-brimmed hat made
from a plate of metal was mounted onto the head of the figure
to preserve the features from injury when being handled.
This can be seen on all genuine apostle spoons, unless of
course they are fake! Apostle spoons, also called 'gossip
spoons', were given to the child by family in-laws, the godparents, or by the old 'gossips' from the village; hence the
name 'gossip spoons'. Wealthy people gave the whole set of
apostle spoons; those of less generosity gave a set of the 'four
evangelists' spoons'. The very poor had to be content to be
able to give or receive just one spoon, which if hand-made,
usually had on the handle a figure that resembled the giver of
the spoon, and were sometimes carved from wood. Such
spoons were given by the child's godparents. If the child was
a boy, the spoon would have been given by the godfather, and
the figure on the handle resembled him; if a girl, the reverse.

Today a full set of genuine apostle spoon would be worth

quite a lot of money and are well worth keeping. Only the other day whilst my father was browsing around our local junk shop he came across an apostle spoon, which incidentally was a very poor imitation. However, the woman who brought it was apparently convinced that for the price of twelve pounds she had found herself a good bargain! As I collect apostle spoons it caught my father's eye, but after looking at it closely, he discovered that the spoon was nothing more than a sterling-silver apostle spoon, well worn, with a badly shaped thick metal oval hat, which had been 'stuck' over the head of the figure on the handle. Presented in a long, black, velvet-lined box, from a distance for a tourist, it would have looked quite fetching, but not the genuine article. But this is not always the case. A few weeks later, my grandmother went into the same shop. Seeing a shoe box on the counter full of old cutlery, she picked out an apostle spoon from amongst the chipped knives and bent forks. The owner was sitting over in the far corner of the shop fixing brass charms to a belt of leather. He called out: 'See anything you like?'

'Yes, how much for this spoon?'

'Did you get it from the box on the counter?'

'Yes.'

'Twenty pence please, love, leave the money by the till.'

On cleaning the spoon, she found that it was hallmarked silver. There isn't a scratch on it, and the spoon itself is a fair weight. In the last century, many shops sold apostle spoons singly, as well as in sets of twelve. Such spoons didn't always have a hat on the handle. So for the price of twenty pence, my grandmother bought a solid silver apostle spoon, which could well be a genuine singular spoon, to add to my collection! Now, that's what I call a bargain. Thanks, gran.

Like many I was given a silver christening spoon with my name engraved on it as a child by my grandmother. But I didn't start collecting Apostle spoons until four years ago. Out of my collection there are two spoons in particular which, to me are priceless and hold a strong sense of 'belonging'. They were given to me by my grandmothers. They were given to them after they had been christened as children. One spoon is sterling-silver, the other is solid silver. The first, was given to my grandmother by her aunt; the second was given to my other grandmother by her godmother. Unfortunately, neither bear a brimmed hat, which would increase their value, but I have no intentions of parting with them, hats or no hats! And even though their only real value is sentimental – never-the-less, I am still proud to own them.

After the Christening

Today very few customs are carried out after the child has been christened; except for 'Wetting the Baby's Head', which has always been a good excuse for the entire family to get together and have a good old booze-up down the local pub. Many 'modern mothers' tend to ignore advice and 'words of wisdom' from the Elders in the family regarding tradition as merely 'old wives' tales', and family customs which have been passed down and carried out through the generations as old 'hocus-pocus!'

The Rubbing of the Heels is an old custom which traditionally should be carried out after the child has been christened (even though some say before). The child's heels are rubbed with a silver coin to bless him or her with luck, fortune and to ensure good health. The coin *must* be kept afterwards, never lost or spent. As long as the coin is kept its power shall remain. If the coin is lost, the child in later life will suffer dire misfortune and will never be 'lucky' in love or successful in business. If the coin is spent, the child will suffer great illness throughout life.

Five years ago, after my friend had given birth to her daughter, Jodie-Ann, I sent her a new fifty pence coin and told her to rub Jodie's heels with it. I stressed that afterwards the coin must be kept, not mislaid, and by no means spent. She had never heard of the custom, and at first she thought that I was joking! However, she assured me that she had done what I asked and that she put the coin away safely in a box.

This particular custom is one which I take very seriously, and like many others mentioned in this book, the 'Rubbing of the Heels' was carried out in my family for years until the death of Louisa, my great grandmother. Sadly, after her death, my own grandmother didn't continue with this family tradition, so much that over the years it has faded and is now lost forever.

I have often given this custom a considerable amount of thought over the years. Due to ill health on Louisa's part, my heels were never rubbed with the coin, that is the coin used to rub each new member of the family. Most of my life I have suffered with my feet, so much that I was confined to a wheelchair for two years.

My sister was born with only 3 toes on her right foot. The fourth toe was just a very small stump, with a tiny nail attached to it. My mother was told by the local nurse that she would have to wear a calliper as soon as she started to walk, and even then, she would never be able to walk properly without the aid of a stick, and she would limp severely for the rest of her life. Miraculously, within a year, her toe started to grow, and by the age of five, it had grown completely. The toe was thin, and looked odd as it had a space either side, but as the years passed, it began to fill out naturally, and now you can't tell the difference between the toes on her right foot and those on her left.

A few months ago, a close friend asked me if I really believed in the superstitions in which I write. To that I smiled and answered 'Yes'.

BIRTH STONES

MONTH	STONE
January	Garnet
February	Amethyst
March	Aquamarine
April	Diamond
May	Emerald
June	Light Amethyst
July	Ruby
August	Peridot
September	Sapphire
October	Rose Zircon
November	Topaz
December	Blue Zircon

FLORAL CALENDAR

MONTH	FLOWER
January	Carnation
February	Violet
March	Daffodil
April	Sweet-peas
May	Lily of the Valley
June	Rose
July	Larkspur
August	Gladioli
September	Aster
October	Marigold
November	Chrysanthemum
December	Narcissus

2   Bird Lore

The familiar call of the cuckoo has made this least-seen bird one of the most loved and well-known birds in Britain. The cuckoo, like many other birds, migrates to Africa during November, returning to Britain in early April or May. For some unknown reason, beyond my knowledge, a cuckoo will always return to the same tree year after year. It is considered extremely lucky to see the bird in full flight on its departure and on its return. The cuckoo is said to sing its first song to the farmers on its arrival telling them that it is time for them to start planting their crops. To a degree, I believe this superstition to be fact. For the last three years now, there has been one particular cuckoo that I have heard (each year on the same day, a Saturday). After it has sung its first song, it flies away (always to the west), then returns to the same spot the following day as though it's keeping a watchful eye on the farmers! The first farmer to hear the first call of the cuckoo is considered to be very highly honoured and will for certain reap a good harvest. Should a farmer hear the first call of the cuckoo whilst planting crops, his harvest will be poor.

Throughout the Midlands, it is an old custom to turn over the money in your pockets on hearing the cuckoo for the first time in Spring. If the cuckoo is heard coming from the direction of your right hand, luck will follow; but if from your left hand the reverse. If you hear the cuckoo for the first time whilst in bed, you shall fall ill before long. (So they say, but I find this a little hard to believe!) When out walking, if you hear a cuckoo calling from woodlands, a grassy meadow, or perched high up in a tree which bears blossom, this symbolizes a long and profitable life ahead. If you hear the bird calling from the direction of a river bank, or waste land, this signifies financial difficulties in the future. If, when out walking, you see a cuckoo perched on an old leaning wooden gate or fence, the foundations of your family life are not as sound as you think they are!

Another old custom is to kiss your right hand and wave it in the direction in which you first heard the bird calling. (If left-handed kiss your left hand). Innocent young fair maidens would run in the direction of the bird's call until it could no longer be heard asking: 'Cuckoo, cuckoo, when shall I be married?' The sick and old folk would patiently bow down asking: 'Cuckoo, cuckoo, when shall I be released from the world's troubles?' How many times the bird sings 'Cuckoo' before flying away signifies how many years will pass. (Some say days or months.)

It is considered most unlucky for a pregnant woman to see a cuckoo. If the bird is perched and silent, it has been said that her child will be born deaf. If the bird is perched and calling, how many times the bird sings 'cuckoo' before taking flight, signifies how many hours the woman will be in labour. Many will argue with this, saying that the bird's call signifies how many children she will have; but I was told as a child that this only applies to a bride if she hears the bird's call whilst making her way to the church.

As a child, when out walking with my grandmother, if a magpie flew near she would salute the bird and say: 'Good morning, Mr Magpie,' or 'Good afternoon' – according to the time of day. Being a child, I would copy her, and the habit has remained with me ever since. I never questioned the reason for this until recently, but she was unable to tell me the significance of saluting one magpie. My grandmother recalls: 'Every Sunday after church, my father and I used to go for a long brisk walk across the common before dinner. If he sighted a magpie he would raise his hat high up above his head (especially if the bird was perched), and then salute the bird. If, whilst walking, he should see a magpie suddenly descend upon the ground, he would spit three times. I would do the same, but out of respect I never questioned his actions.' Putting her knitting aside, she hastily added, 'Of course, father would never permit me to spit, such behaviour was unheard of!'

Not totally satisfied, and determined to find out the significance of saluting one magpie I telephoned my other grandmother who was able to tell me the reason for this old family superstition.

'To see one magpie is a bad omen, especially if the bird is not in full flight. The magpie is considered to be an evil bird, the raising of the hat is by no means done as a sign of respect for the bird. The hat is, as they say "raised up to Heaven" and by saluting, you are directing the evil away from yourself back to the bird which will then take flight, thus taking away with it any bad luck that may have descended upon you.' (To spit removes or prevents a curse).

Well, that did certainly shed some light upon the matter, but didn't explain why my grandmother was always so polite to a bird which is considered to be evil and unlucky! I put this question to her only the other day, and knowing my grand-mother, I should have had some idea as to the logical explanation in her reply. 'When you were small, to teach you the names of the birds, when out walking if a wren flew near I would say: 'Good morning Jenny Wren', or if a robin I would say, 'Good morning Cock Robin', the same applied to the magpie. You would copy what I had said, it gave you an interest in birds and helped you to identify them. It also made our walks pleasurable and fun. I would point to a bird, and if you got the name right I'd give you a sweet, how many sweets you got depended on how many birds you named correctly.'

This harmless superstitious act of saluting one magpie has got me into many embarrassing situations on several occa-sions. Here is one incident which I can remember only too well! I was sitting in the dentist's chair having a brace fitted. The dentist was working from behind me chatting away (as they invariably do). His assistant was standing beside me holding a metal tray. I caught sight of a magpie outside the window. Acting upon impulse, I immediately saluted the bird with my right hand and in the process I knocked the tray right out of her hands. It fell crashing to the floor along with all its contents and the mouth wash went flying across the room. I tried to explain my actions and apologize for the mess I had made, but unlike the dentist, she didn't see the funny side of it at all. She stamped around the room muttering loudly under her breath. The main reason she was so annoyed was because she had only just sterilized the instruments, and as

I was the first patient, she had to go and sterilize them again. She did get rather wet and didn't have another white coat to change into as the one she was wearing was stained pink!

If you listen to idle gossip you could be easily taken for a ride by thieves!

Never leave hair ribbons about, for should a magpie pick them up and use them to feather her nest, long life will not be yours!

Magpies are reknowned for being great hoarders. They are attracted to brightly coloured objects, in particular wool, material and ribbon as the above superstition suggests. My sister has always hoarded all manner of useless things. She can't bear to throw anything away, the mere thought of it leaves her feeling hot and flustered. Her idea of a good sort out is to pull all the 'rubbish' out from underneath her bed, re-arrange it into different boxes and containers, then put it all back again! Amongst the badges, keyrings, bangles, toys, and a huge mountain of magazines lie enough pens, pencils, rubbers, and paper to supply W.H. Smith's for a year! I nicknamed my sister 'Maggie Magpie' when she was a child (and to her annoyance) I still call her 'Maggie' to this day. At the age of three, she was broken hearted when a magpie flew down and stole her new shiny gold pencil, which she had left outside on the window ledge. We were sitting at the dining-room table having our evening meal when the cheeky bird quickly flew down and took it right before her eyes.

I can remember running home from school one day feeling very pleased with myself, clutching tightly in my hands a 'Dolly-Peg' that I had made in art class. The teacher had already painted on a face, and glued on black wool for hair, so all I had to do was make the clothes. I picked out of the scrap-box a white spotted hanky which I made into a pop over dress, and from a square of red felt I cut out a cloak, and a simple triangle for a head-scarf, and glued them on. A few days later, I helped my grandmother hang out the washing, and proudly used my 'Dolly-Peg' to peg one of my socks onto the line. During the afternoon the heavens opened, and it poured down with rain. As it was a fair walk from the house to the washing lines, my gran wouldn't let me run across to get it. While I looked out of the window, praying for the rain

to stop, suddenly, from out of nowhere, a magpie swooped
down and flew off with my peg! I yelled and banged on the
window, and as you can imagine, being only a small child
there were tears and tantrums. I didn't blame the bird, I
blamed my grandmother for not allowing me to go and get it!
I can remember teasing my sister when she was in floods of
tears, but my laughter soon stopped when my mother re-
minded me of my little episode, and how I reacted!

Old Rhyme:

> See one for sorrow, two for mirth,
> Three for a death, and four for a birth.

The more commonly known Magpie Rhyme:

> One for sorrow, two for joy,
> Three for a girl, four for a boy.
> Five for silver, six for gold,
> Seven for a secret never to be told.
> Eight for a lover, nine for a kiss,
> Ten for good fortune, a spell, or a wish.

Some events are lucky and others definitely unlucky. Fortune, past or present, good or bad can be foretold in the
simplest things that surround us. Here is a short section on
using birds to foretell good fortune or bad luck.

If a bride sees many birds in full flight as she makes her way
to the church to be married, she will have many strong and
handsome children. To see any bird fly in at an open window
is unlucky, but if the bird flew out quicker than it flew in, no
mishap need be feared.

The cockerel (especially the black cock) is one bird that has
always been connected with witchcraft and many superstitions. It is known to many as the 'sun bird', and is considered
to be the enemy of all ghosts and spirits. The cock is said to
have crowed at the exact time of the birth of Jesus Christ and
according to legend, on the last day, when God will descend
upon a cloud from the Heavens above, every cock will crow
to awaken the dead, including both wooden and metal weather-
vanes which can be seen on towers and church spires throughout

the town and countryside. It was once thought that if a freshly killed cockerel was buried underneath the foundations of a newly-built church it would keep out the Devil, protect the congregation from evil, and its blood would purify the earth preventing disease. A cock crowing at midnight means a departing soul has been claimed. If a cock crows three times at midnight, the 'angel of death' has come himself! A crowing cock facing the house door foretells a stranger is coming. A crowing hen will bring nothing but bad luck to the owner. If you dream of a cockerel crowing, someone you trust and regard as a friend is talking about your most inner secrets and ambitions. If in your dream you see a beautiful coloured cockerel, a profitable idea which you have been considering needs to be set in motion before you meet with competition. To dream of a hen sitting on her eggs (like the crane and the stork) symbolizes family and the birth of a child, but not necessarily your own. If whilst out walking you see many hens, this is a good sign for you to sort out family situations, and improve your life financially.

To see two crows fly near or over your house is a bad sign. It is also unlucky to see a crow standing on one leg! For some unknown reason beyond my knowledge, crows have been connected with money over the years as you will see from the following superstitions:

To see a crow during the summer months is lucky, money that has been invested will reward you well. To sight a crow during winter is unlucky, especially if the bird is perched and cawing, the inactivity of the bird is a warning to pull out of any moneymaking scheme which you have recently become involved in for it will bring you little profit, if any! To hear a crow cawing in a dream is equally unlucky where money is concerned. The dreamer can expect to hear bad news about a project which at first seemed to be a good and profitable idea. When you hear a crow caw, place one foot before the other to measure your own shadow by your footsteps. Count these steps, add thirteen, then divide the total by six. If the remaining number is one, you can expect good luck. If two, bad luck is awaiting you. Three foretells happiness, four plenty of rich food, and five foretells money in the future.

Like the magpie, the crow, jackdaw, nightjar, raven, and

rook have always been associated with witchcraft, magic, and the devil. These birds were thought to be servants of Satan, and were called the six spies of 'evil doings'. The nightjar is considered to be the most evil bird out of the six. It has the power, if its master permits, to claim the soul of any unchristened child. It can also take the form of any animal in order to roam the earth to carry out the devil's instructions. Curiously enough, there are many who believe that when we leave this world we are reincarnated and return as a bird. (I am a very open-minded person, but if there is any truth in reincarnation, I would rather return as myself for one very simple reason, I hate cats!)

To dream of a bird (especially if black), signifies bad luck and misfortune. To dream of a nightjar signifies illness; to dream of this bird whilst severely ill signifies death, your own.

(I do not adhere to the above superstitions, I have merely included them out of interest only.)

To see any one of these six birds is indeed a bad omen, especially if seen before going on a journey, but any misfortune will be reversed if a martin, robin, or a wren is sighted soon afterwards.

According to a well-known superstition, if the ravens that guard the crown jewels in the Tower of London should leave, the jewels would be stolen and the tower itself would crumble to dust!

Rooks are said to leave a rookery when the last owner of the house or land dies, but they won't leave until after the funeral, when the owner is at rest. Even then, one rook will attend the graveyard to pay its last respects before all the birds leave the old rookery. Rooks can often be seen perched on old headstones; perhaps they return yearly to their owner's resting place, paying respect, or casting torment? Like many things in folklore, one will never really know!

To hear an owl hooting at night brings news of a death. It is considered to be an 'Omen of Death' should an owl perch on your chimney. To dream of an owl signifies disappointment and the loss of a friend if the dreamer sees the owl flying away from him. An old and rather cruel superstition says that if an owl enters your house, it should be killed at once. If it is released, the bird will fly away with the house's good fortune. To hear an owl hooting and circling above you in a dream is a useful warning to ignore vicious gossip from so-called friends and colleagues, and to continue with whatever you have decided upon. You will rise above others, and achieve your goal.

There is sure to be a death in the family if a white pigeon should perch on top of your house. Mark the date and month, and remember it well! To dream of a pigeon foretells good news from afar: if the bird is flying towards you, you can expect a letter from a friend you haven't seen for a long time. To see many pigeons flying towards your house in a dream indicates that distant relations will soon pay you an unexpected visit.

Old Saying:

> He that harms the robin or the wren
> Will never prosper on land or at sea,
> And will never be blessed with children.

The cheerful little robin is probably one of the most loved, well known birds throughout the British Isles. The robin is indeed a very lucky little bird, and I failed to find any superstition which associated the robin with any kind of misfortune or bad luck except for the following: it is very unlucky to kill a robin, even the mere thought of harming the bird in any way will bring bad luck upon the owner. It seems that even cats respect this particular superstition as cats tend to steer clear and rarely harm them! Although not mentioned in the scriptures, one legend in folklore foretells how the robin acquired its beautiful red breast. On the first Good Friday (the day of Christ's crucifixion), when Jesus wore his crown of thorns, a robin flew down from the dark skies and tried to remove a thorn from his forehead, and in doing so, his chest was stained with Christ's blood. To see a robin on Good Friday is extremely lucky. It is a fact that a robin's breast will appear to be 'blood red' at Christmas, so perhaps there is some truth in this legend after all! Young robins do not acquire their familiar red breast until late August, so they often go around unnoticed. This confuses people who assume that robins are born with a red breast. The cheerful little robin with its beautiful scarlet breast, whose song fills the air like the smell of a delicate, sweet perfume, is one of my favourite birds, and any traditional Christmas country scene would be incomplete without its presence.

3 Country Lore

When I was a child, my grandmother would warn me: 'Never pick and eat the blackberries on October the eleventh, the Devil has cursed them!'

I never used to take any notice of what she had said, that is, until after I had eaten them. With my hands and mouth stained purplish black, I would wash my hands and face in the stream, then hunt for a lily to rub on to my skin in a desperate attempt to remove the evidence. I wasn't scared of what my grandmother would do to me when I got home, because she didn't believe in unnecessary smacking, I did it because I used to feel so guilty for going against her word. She'd take one look at me, laugh, and say, 'You've got the cheek of the Devil, go and have a good wash before your mother comes home!'

According to legend, when God cast Lucifer, prince of darkness and master of all evil, out of Heaven, he fell spinning through space down to earth where he landed in a blackberry bush. Satan, or Old Nick, as he is sometimes called, is said to have an extremely long memory. He can't forgive, and he most certainly never forgets, and for this reason, each years he spits on to the blackberries making them unfit for us to eat, thus marking the anniversary of his fall. I personally believe that there is a degree of truth in this old superstition. It is written in the scriptures: 'And he said unto them, I beheld Satan as lightning fall from Heaven.' (Luke 10 v18). The Devil is said to tempt us from walking the righteous path of life, and in a sense that is exactly what he does when the blackberries are concerned. The biggest, ripest, mouth-watering berries are always high up, surrounded by thorns, and out of arm's reach. Yet greed, and the mere fact that we can't have them simply because we can't reach them, makes them more desirable. But whether he did actually land in a blackberry bush is doubtful and beyond belief, and like so many other things in life, one will never know!

Bramble Cures

An ancient custom known throughout Gloucestershire to cure young boys suffering from ruptures is to pass the child backwards and forwards through an arch made from brambles.

To my knowledge bramble cures are still carried out today, especially in the West Country. Anyone known to be suffering with boils or a bad skin disease is made to crawl underneath the brambles, either willingly or by force! To refuse, will bring shame upon the child's family, and sickness throughout the land. It is considered to be extremely lucky to crawl under a bramble bush, although I personally wouldn't advise it!

Cows have been known to be dragged through a bramble arch to cure paralysis. One particular summer, my grandfather witnessed this most unusual performance. All the villagers gathered around the arch to watch the ritual take place. The women brought food and drink, and the younger children played in a field nearby. After a few brief moments of whispers and deep conversation, everyone clapped and cheered as the reluctant cow was led into the field by four farmers. A halter was thrown around the cow's neck whilst a young farm hand quickly ran and closed the gate. The two men in front pulled hard on the rope, and two men pushed the cow from behind. Eventually, after five hours the poor demented animal was dragged through the bramble arch. After a great stir of excitement and various cries of laughter, the farmers, looking very satisfied with themselves, made their way down the steep hill to the village pub to celebrate the success of the passing through the bramble arch.

Farmers fear deformed animals being born on their land as it is considered to be a bad omen. The local superstition is that unless the deformed animal is taken off the farm and killed at once, there will be a death. This old superstition came about many years ago when a farmer had a deformed calf born on his land. The newly-born calf had two heads and six legs. All the farmhands and the vet who were present at the birth ran away in horror and left the calf alive. The next day the farmer was found dead in the milking shed. They were convinced that he was cursed because the calf was born on his land and allowed to live.

Old local saying:

> Freaks a-being born you dread,
> Kill them else tomorrow you be dead.

Farmers used to plant holly trees on their land to protect their cattle from any evil, and to prevent them from being struck by lightning. They also believed that the wood of the tree when thrown at any animal had the power to make the animal return and lie down beside it. In fact, the bark was said to maintain such power that when thrown, it didn't even have to touch the beast in order to make it retreat.

The holly tree, when planted by a cottage, was thought to be a protection to ward off witches. A holly wreath affixed to a wooden door or window will keep one safe from evil, and repel witches. These superstitions, like many others, are old pagan customs. The wreath itself is symbolic as it represents the crown of thorns that Christ wore on the day of his crucifixion. For this reason the holly tree is also called 'christ thorn' or the 'holy' tree. Legend has it that the holly tree sprung up from underneath Christ's footsteps when he first walked the earth.

Local Superstition

The holly tree is regarded as sacred and must never be cut down. Its branches may be trimmed, but no axe is permitted to touch the bark of the tree, and the roots must never be removed from the ground.

Old Saying:

> Take an axe to a holly tree,
> Sickness and death shall fall upon thee.

We were told the above superstition when we first moved into our house. We had to promise that we would never cut down the holly tree which stands to the side of the cottage amongst the elder trees. We were also asked by the previous owners that if ever we were to move, we would tell the new occupants about this old village lore.

One year my father attempted to move the tree slightly, as it stands directly in front of the French windows and in the summer it blocks out most of the sunlight. In doing so he fell down an old well! Luckily, all that was hurt was his pride. The tree itself is older than the cottage, its roots lie deep beneath the foundations of the house, which was built on farmland at the end of the 17th century. Some of the villagers (mostly farming folk) are still superstitious. They believe that if a holly tree is cut down, and its roots removed from the earth, death, doom, and destruction will sweep through the village.

Over the years we have become very fond of the tree and no longer refer to it as an eye-sore. In fact it has great character, and as the tree was there many years before we came on the scene, it has the right to remain where it is. We are led to believe that the holly tree was placed exactly where it still stands today to mark the boundary line of the stream, which was used to divide the surrounding land.

Every year, around late November, my father carefully trims the holly tree, and from the branches makes a wreath to hang on the front door at Christmas. In making the wreath he always pricks his fingers and a few drops of blood fall onto the leaves. This is said to be very lucky, the owner will have good health throughout the new year to come. However, this is of little comfort to my father when adding the finishing touches with plasters on his fingers and muttering under his breath certain words that for obvious reasons I cannot print! Any branches that are left over are thrown away, never burnt on the fire, for the wood of the holly tree is regarded as sacred like the Holy Bible itself. To burn the wood signifies death of all that is good and pure, and is considered to be an act of denial against God.

Like the holly, it is most unlucky to burn the wood of the elder. There are many superstitions and legends connected with the elder. One of the most famous claims that in the branches of the tree dwells Hyldle-Mœr the elder tree's mother, or the 'tree spirit' who lives inside the tree and watches over it. Should the tree be cut down, and furniture be made from the wood, Hyldle-Moer will follow her property, and haunt the owners till death.

It was an old Gloucestershire custom to trim an elder bush into the shape of a cross and plant it on a newly-dug grave. If the bush blossomed the next year, the soul of the person beneath was happy. Many refer to the elder as the 'tree of death' and consider it to be an unlucky tree to sit or walk under. It is also known as the 'Judas tree' after Judas Iscariot who betrayed Jesus. After Jesus's body was delivered to Pontius Pilate, Judas repented and brought back the thirty pieces of silver he had been paid to the chief priests and elders, saying he had sinned and betrayed the innocent blood. When he was ignored, he cast down the pieces of silver in the temple and went out and hanged himself. (Matthew 27:3–5) Although it doesn't actually say in the scriptures, folklore has it he hanged himself on an elder tree, which would account for the name given to the tree and the superstition surrounding it.

Hazel is also considered a very unlucky wood to burn, as its branches are able to find hidden water beneath the ground. The familiar saying, 'Fire, fire quench water' has probably helped to rekindle this old belief. If you build a fire of hazel in a new grate, no other wood will ever burn, and you can expect nothing but ashes and earth from the water pump. A forked twig of hazel was made into a divining-rod, as it had the power to seek out witches. It was used in water divining, and also to detect buried treasure. T.J. Hutchinson in his book *Two Years In Peru*, tells of a carved figure in a rock bearing a forked rod. From archaeological reports it is estimated that Peruvian civilizations date back before 9000 BC. No doubt the power of divination was only used by the magicians and sorcerers of that time.

The rod as we know it today did not become an established art until the sixteenth century. However, there is one exception: a brief whisper of it in a manuscript dated 1430 written by a mine surveyor. In Sweden, the dowser was called a *Dalkarl*. A Swedish twelfth century manuscript says that the *Dalkarl* should find a mountain ash which was grown from a seed dropped out of a bird's beak. Then, at twilight, between the third day and night after Lady Day he should break off a twig. Next, he should bring the twig into contact with iron or steel, making sure not to let it fall to the ground. At that point the rod is ready for various magical purposes. In Denmark, it is claimed lost treasures can be discovered with a magic rod called the *Finkelrut*, which is cut during St John's night, while invoking the Christian trinity. The *Finkelrut* may also be used for finding water but only if it is made from a willow branch and operated by a man born under Aquarius. Another fascinating note regarding the *Finkelrut*: in arms of the ancient Danish family of Bille, there is a figure of a troll holding a sapling. Tradition has it that during the dry season such a troll came with a sapling in his hands and found water.[1]

Witchhazel was chosen by the Saxons for their temples, the hazel being one of Thor's trees. The first Christian church in England was built in Glastonbury of wattles of hazel. In Sweden, oats that are fed to horses are first touched with a hazel bough as a protection against the evil eye. It is also believed in Sweden that he who eats the hazel nuts will become invisible, and the nuts are used in divination on Nutcrack Night, on All Hallow's Eve. It was with a hazel bough that St Patrick drove the snakes out of Ireland. All folklorists agree about the magical and protective virtues of the tree. In Germany the hazel tree is known as *Zauber-Strauch*, which means the 'magic tree'.[2]

The rowan, also known as mountain ash or 'witch wood', was also considered an unlucky wood to burn. An old superstition advises, never sit around a fire if this wood is burning, for whom you sit with shall prove to be your enemies before long! But this may not be so if rosemary is also burning in the grate, for rosemary induces love and opens all hearts, especially those of men. My grandmother once told me that her aunt wouldn't even allow the wood near the wood-pile, let alone in the house, and that she would rather burn her best chair than stack the fire with rowan. If an iron poker is placed

---

[1] Greg Nielsen & Joseph Polansky, *Pendulum Power*, Aquarian Press, 1977.
[2] See also my book, *An English Rose*, Ashgrove Press, 1990.

upright against the bars of a sulking fire, it will drive away the Devil from the hearth.

During the 16th century, country folk would pick witch elm and witchhazel in secret, for if a stranger should happen to see them it was believed that bad luck would befall the village: And no doubt, ignorant villagers would brand them as witches. When bloom and fruit are seen together on an oak apple tree, it is said to be a sign that there will be a death in the owner's house before long. Take an oak apple from an oak tree and open it; if you find an insect within, watch it very carefully: If the insect quickly flies away, then war is near; if it slowly creeps inside the apple, corn will be scarce and bread dear; if it turns around, there will be a great sickness in the land from whence you picked the apple. This is very old country land lore.

The noble St Dunstan had many orchards and used to supply the local inns with his cider. However, one year most of his apple trees were destroyed by the frost, and what was left made very little poor cider. He became insanely jealous of the local farmers who had managed to produce a good cider. According to legend, he sold his soul to the Devil and signed a covenant in blood. In return for his soul, the Devil promised him that each year he would send a frost on the 17th, 18th and 19th May to destroy every apple tree laden with blossom for miles around, so that his cider would be the best throughout the land, as his apple trees wouldn't be affected by the frost.

Farmers considered it very unlucky to cut the last sheaf of the harvest so they were made into corn dolls. The dolls would then be dressed and garlanded and carried home in procession (usually by the children), and either kept in the house or the village church throughout the year to ensure a good harvest the following year. This custom, like so many others is a survival of Pagan rites originating from the Middle East over 7000 years ago. This tradition when carried out appeased the Corn Spirit or the Fertility Goddess, who took her final refuge in the last sheaf.

Corn dolls are made in many different elaborate shapes and traditional patterns which vary from village to village. There are many different names given to each doll, such as the Kirn Baby, Mare, Maiden, and the Hag. The Staffordshire Knot, the

Suffolk Horseshoe, and the Northamptonshire Horn of Plenty, are just three of the many typical goodluck dolls that are still made and sold today.

Any farm would be incomplete without a cat.

The cat is highly respected and is of great use to the farmer. Ever since farmers realized its use as a vermin controller (which was probably in Saxon times), the domestic cat has found itself a secure place in the barn or at the fireside. It has been estimated that each rat will cause over £3 worth of damage a year. The average farm cat will kill over 250 rats a year, making the cat a vital farm animal as well as the family pet. There are many superstitions connected with the cat, black cats in particular, but surprisingly enough all are good, which I find somewhat strange and confusing as for centuries black cats have always been associated with witches. Even the sight of a black cat is lucky! If whilst out walking a black cat should happen to cross your path you will succeed in business. If a black cat enters your house good luck is said to come in with it. The animal should not be driven away but welcomed in and fed. To cure any swelling of the eye, rub it with the tail of a black cat three times! To see a black cat before going on a journey is lucky, and better still if sighted on your return. If a black cat sneezes and all the family is present, a cold will run through the family. (So perhaps not so lucky after all!)

To see a white cat is considered to be very unlucky, even though white has always been connected with good, 'white magic'. My grandmother advises: 'If you see a white cat, look away, and if by chance you happen to see a black cat, you will have nothing to fear.' White cats are said to be deaf, and to a degree this is true. White cats that have blue eyes and pure white fur, without the slightest trace of black, are actually born deaf and remain so for about 3–5 weeks after being born, and sometimes, if after 5 weeks they do not obtain hearing, they will remain deaf. However, this is rare. According to legend, the witch cursed the white cat because it refused to listen to any evil spells!

It is unlucky to see a white cat before entering a church, especially if you are to be married. It is also unlucky to see a white cat on your birthday. If you see a white cat rubbing itself against a tree, it won't be long before someone rubs you up the wrong way. If a white cat enters your garden watch it carefully; when it has gone retrace its steps, sprinkling salt on the ground as you do so.

The horse, unlike the cat, has not always been a farm animal. In fact, it wasn't until the early 18th century that the horse replaced the ox for farming purposes. Until the tractor came along, farmers used the horse for ploughing for 200 years. Even today, some farmers still use the horse for ploughing, especially the shire, as it is a good, strong, sturdy horse. Indeed, the horse was of great value to the farmer and had to be carefully looked after: not only groomed, fed, and housed, but also protected against sickness and evil. To protect the horse from evil, the farmer would affix brass charms to the horse's harness. The most commonly used brass horse charms of the 18th century was a semi-closed circle which had a small bell in the middle. When attached to the brow band, the bell would ring as the horse walked, frightening away any evil spirits. Other brass charms that were used to ward off evil were the designs of the three moons, the sun, and the stars.

Brass charms are still affixed to the harness but purely for decoration. Most of those that can be seen today are the modern descendants of the original primitive charms that were used long ago.

A circle with a bunch of wheatsheaf in the middle is one of the five original charms against evil and is still a very popular charm today. I do not own a horse, but nevertheless I have a wheatsheaf charm amongst many others above the fireplace.

A horseshoe has always been greatly regarded as a symbol of good luck. A horseshoe should never be polished, as by doing so you are rubbing away its power. Once a horseshoe has been affixed above a dwelling, it should never be removed. You should always affix a horseshoe upturned, never pointing downwards, that is unless you want the luck to run out! A horseshoe when placed correctly above a dwelling will keep good fortune in and violent spirits out.

In a small village in Suffolk, a blacksmith is said to have been protected from evil influences and witchcraft as he had an upturned horseshoe nailed above the forge. Other blacksmiths who didn't have a horseshoe nailed above the forge were victims of strange experiences which couldn't be explained. Fires suddenly started in the dead of night, tools disappeared, and any horse that went near to the forge would stampede in sheer terror. The local vicar was sent for, who blessed the forges, and affixed the horseshoes above the dwellings himself. As soon as he had left the strange goings-on stopped!

Unlike the cat, a white horse is lucky, and to see a horse that has four white legs is indeed a fortunate omen! But bad luck is sure to follow if you meet, own, or buy a horse that has one, two or three white legs. When you see a pure white horse close your eyes and make a wish, then look around and if by chance you see a girl with red hair, your wish will be granted. This old gypsy superstition is one which I have put to the test many times. During the summer, the farmer's wife often rides by my cottage on a beautiful big white horse. However, the chance of seeing a girl with red hair is most unlikely, simply because there isn't anyone at our end of the village with red hair, but I make a wish all the same!

Clover has always been associated with good luck. It is lucky to find a four-leaved clover in England, or in Ireland, a four-leaved shamrock. A three-leaved clover is linked with the 'Holy Trinity'. When found, it will bring good luck, health and will also repel witches. In some parts, to find a two-leaved clover promises wealth. In other parts of the country, it is considered unlucky. To find a four-leaved clover is indeed very lucky. It will bring instant luck, induce love, and it is said to give the finder the gift of second sight to enable the possessor to see fairies, elves and goblins. It has the power to detect witches, and will keep one safe from evil.

Old Rhyme:

> One leaf for fame, and two for wealth
> The third shall bring you splendid health,
> The fourth shall bring you a faithful lover,
> This is the luck of the four leaved clover.
> If two people eat a two leaved clover together,
> Friends they shall remain forever and ever.

It is unlucky to see three butterflies together. A strange and rather old superstition says that one ought to kill the first of these lovely things when seen in Spring.

The cheerful little cricket is indeed a lucky little fellow and should never be killed. If a cricket should hop into your house, good luck will follow it. There are a number of other insects that are supposed to be lucky such as the red and black spotted ladybird. When my father finds a ladybird in the garden he quickly puts it on to his prize rose tree, as they eat the black and green flies.

> Ladybird, ladybird fly away home,
> Your house is on fire, and your children all gone.

When I was a child, I used to pull their wings off so that they couldn't fly away. I did this because once I had found a ladybird and put it into a matchbox, my folks would make me let it go. I can still hear my mother's voice saying, 'Selena, let the poor thing out of that box, it's cruel.' When I think about it, keeping a ladybird for a few days in a matchbox isn't half as cruel as pulling its wings off! Snails are said to be lucky, although I can't think why! 'Step on a snail and you'll be sorry,' my gran used to say.

Spiders are said to be very lucky. My father has never once killed a spider, much to my mother's annoyance, as living in an old cottage, we were overrun with spiders. She's forever sweeping cobwebs away from the fireplace and the wooden stairs. Country spiders are far bigger than we are used to, being town folk. Hardly a night passes without my mother giving out a loud scream, 'Kill it, kill it,' she yells at my dad, but he never does. He traps it in a jam jar and puts it outside the front door, then it runs back in again, back to its usual place under the stairs.

Not only are spiders considered to be lucky but useful too. A freshly spun cobweb when applied to an open wound will help to stop the bleeding. If a cobweb isn't at hand, a fresh yarrow leaf will serve just as well as yarrow contains a substance which will help to clot the flowing of blood. Parkinson tells us that: 'If it be put into the nose, assuredly it will stay the bleeding of it.' In the Eastern counties, yarrow is termed 'Yarroway' and there is a curious mode of divination with its serrated leaf, with which the inside of the nose is tickled while the following lines are spoken. If the operation causes the nose to bleed, it is a certain omen of success:

> Yarroway, Yarroway, bear a white blow,
> If my love love me, my nose will bleed now.

It was one of the herbs dedicated to the Evil One, in earlier days, being known as Devil's Nettle, Devil's Plaything, Bad Man's Plaything, and was used for divination in spells.[3]

Yarrow, also known as 'Nose-Bleed' can be found growing in hedgerows or on waste ground. It has been used for hundreds of years by country folk, being a good all round herb, used to treat anything from a common cold to an oily complexion. However, this useful herb will creep its way into gardens, it is loved by many but is a nightmare to proud gardeners. A poultice made from yarrow leaves and toadflax applied outwardly will induce sleep, ease pain, and help to reduce bleeding. In Scotland an ointment is still made from the leaves and is applied to open sores and ulcers. Yarrow is indeed a very useful herb and has many other medicinal uses: it will reduce high blood pressure and heal bleeding piles. It is an excellent blood purifier, and when taken as a tea will help in the early stages of a cold. It was also given to children to help aid sleep. Every herb has a place in folklore and superstition and yarrow is no exception. The following is a delightful spell which I simply could not exclude.

An ounce of yarrow sewed up in flannel and placed under the pillow before going to bed, having repeated the following words, brought a vision of the future husband or wife:

> Thou pretty herb of Venus' tree,
> Thy true name it is Yarrow;
> Now who my bosom friend must be,
> Pray tell thou me to-morrow'[4]
> (Halliwell's Popular Rhymes, etc.)

An old country herb superstition says that a bunch of fresh

---

[3] & [4] Mrs M. Grieve *Old Herbal*, published by Jonathan Cape, 1931.

yarrow leaves when hung over the door of the garden shed will protect the tools from being stolen.

Another country herb superstition is to hang up a bunch of deadly nightshade over the pig's trough. However, this isn't merely superstition, this is a proven remedy to prevent the swine against fever. It has never failed, or so I've been told. (Great care needs to be taken as this is a very poisonous herb).

The deadly nightshade (*atropoa belladonna*), was named after Atropos, who according to Greek mythology was the eldest of the 'Three Fates', Atropos, Clotho and Lachesis, who governed human destinies. Clotho spun the thread of life, Lachesis worked happiness, love and sorrow into it, and Atropos cut the thread of man's life with her fatal shears at the time appointed for death.

The word *belladonna* probably comes from the Italian women as they used it to make the eyes lustrous by dropping a little of the extracted juice of the berries into the eyes to dilate and enlarge the pupils. The deadly nightshade is also known as dwale, a word of 'doom' which comes from the Latin word *delere* which means to suffer. I personally like the herb, and find it most attractive even though it is the most harmful of all our poisonous herbs. A 'Furious and deadly plant. Not one of our British plants is so deadly as this,' wrote Anne Pratt. 'It will never be allowed to become really familiar for the same reason that a man would not give his children prussic acid to play shop.' (Old Herbal, 1931).

My great uncle's first wife, Ellen, who worked for a publishing business, often complained of a chesty cough and thought that it was due to being constantly around print. One Monday morning, when she arrived at work, instead of going into the office, she went into the firm's private gymnasium to limber up as she was feeling sluggish. Whilst exercising she haemorrhaged and was rushed to hospital, where T.B. was diagnosed. She was then sent to a sanitorium, but as there was no improvement, and in those days no known cure, she was administered belladonna which left her blind and shortly afterwards she died. However, this most feared plant is widely used today in both homoeopathic and modern medicine. Belladonna linaments are used to help such disorders as rheumatism and gout. It is also used successfully to treat asthma, influenza and other chest complaints. When used correctly, the deadly nightshade is a very useful and important herb, although not many would agree unless they know and respect the medicinal properties of this herb.

The berries when ripe look similar to the blackberry, being a deep purple black in colour, and very sweet looking. Legend has it that an evil elf purposely made them to resemble the blackberry to lure and entice poor innocent children to their fate, hence the country name for the berry, 'the cherry of death.' A certain aura of magic has always surrounded this plant in particular, and it is said that any witch's 'midnight brew' would be incomplete without it.

Country folk have used the berries for dyeing clothing for centuries, they also used flowers, plants, leaves and bark to obtain the colour they required. A mordant such as alum or sodium was added to the dyeing water to help bind the colour to the cloth for a longer-lasting effect. Of course shop-bought dyes are far easier to use but the process of the actual dyeing is the same, the only advantage being that you don't have to go wandering through woodlands to gather the berries or plants to prepare the dye. Long ago, dyeing was carried out in many households, and was considered no more tiresome than leading the grate. Dyeing your own clothes is interesting, creative and fun, and furthermore it won't cost you a penny.

Dyeing clothing with natural substances is rewarding and simple as long as you follow a few basic rules, much as you would expect to read on a shop-bought chemical dye (well, almost). You can't go wrong. So now you have decided to take the plunge and give it a go; have fun, and good luck!

Basic Tips for Dyeing

1. Having chosen an article of clothing to dye, select a colour from the list given.
2. Collect the necessary plants, flowers, berries, etc. Boil on a high heat for as long as possible to extract the colour. Strain several times. Add a mordant if needed.
3. Use rain or bottled water for dyeing and rinsing – not tap water.

4. The dyeing pot must be wide enough to allow the cloth to circulate without tangling.
5. Use an iron or steel pot to dye dark colours, and copper for light.
6. Make sure that the cloth is clean. Wash in cold water first before fully immersing into the dyeing water. Allow to simmer slowly for 45 minutes to three hours. (The longer left to simmer the stronger the colour will be.)
7. Rinse well until water runs clear. Hang out to dry.

If you have never used this method of dyeing before, to avoid disappointment it's best to start off dyeing small things such as handkerchiefs, tee-shirts, or shorts, before attempting skirts, dresses and jumpers. You never know, it could turn out to be a new and fascinating pasttime. You will notice that the list contains American spellings. I purposely left it as it was written for originality. Many of the plants listed are the same as ours, only we know them by different names, for example, 'bluebottle's blooms' are cornflowers (*centaurea cyanus*), better known to us as 'blue caps.'[5]

Plant Boiled	Add	Resulting Color
Sassafras	Alum (2 tbsp to 1 lb. cloth)	Soft Yellow Tan
Blue Bottles (blooms)	Alum	Blue
Broomsedge	Alum	Yellow
Cocklebur	Alum	Chartreuse
Butternut	Copperas (1 tbsp)	Medium Brown
Pecan Hulls	Alum	Tan
Black Walnut Hulls	None	Brown (stains wood)
White Oak Bark	None	Chartreuse
Sourwood	Walnut Hulls	Black
Apple Tree Bark	Alum	Dark Yellow Tan
Madder	Alum	Red; Scarlet
Tobacco	Alum and Cream of Tartar (1 tbsp)	Tan
Hickory Bark	Alum	Yellow

[5] Ferne Shelton, *Pioneer Comforts and Kitchen Remedies*, Hutcraft, N.C., 1965.

Maple Bark	Vinegar and Cream of Tartar	Rose Tan
Cochineal	Alum	Rose; Red
Arbor Vitae	None	Green
Onion Skins (dried)	Alum	Yellow
Smooth Sumac (stems)	None	Yellow
Dahlia Blooms	Alum and Cream of Tartar	Yellow
Jewel Weed	Few rusty nails	Yellow
Morning Glory Blooms	Alum and Cream of Tartar	Yellow
Yellow Dock (root)	Mesquite gum	Yellow
Zinnia Blossoms	Alum and Cream of Tartar	Yellow (Indians)
Alder (bark)	None	Brown
Golden Rod	Alum	Yellow
Puccoon roots	Oak Bark	Red
Rhododendron leaves	Copperas (1 tbsp)	Gray
Strawberry Fruit	(Rubbed on)	Red; Pink (Indians)
Marigold Blooms	Alum	Deep Yellow
Sunflower Petals	Alum and Cream of Tartar	Yellow
Poke Berries	Vinegar	Red (fades)
Privet Leaves	Alum and Cream of Tartar	Yellow
Sumac Berries	Copperas	Dark Gray
Tulip Tree Leaves	Alum	Yellow
Indigo	Alum and Cream of Tartar	Blue
Lily of the Valley (leaves) (No Mordant)	Alum	Yellow

4 Weather Lore

For centuries man has possessed ideas as to the mystery of the weather. Through the years many strange and different techniques have been used to forecast and control the weather. The Vikings stood with raised hands to hear and obey Odin, the most powerful of all Gods; Indians drew symbols in the soil enclosed in a circle, and danced to hear and carry out the wishes of Rain Spirits. They used different methods of dance, one to bring rain, one to stop it. Other tribes sacrificed young virgins to appease the Sun God.

Ever since Noah sent the Dove to find land after the flood, birds have been used as weather prophets. Farmers forecast the weather by observing birds, their animals, or by the natural things that surround them such as trees and plants. Here are a few examples on using birds as weather prophets which were told to me by a local farmer. Ducks rushing around flapping their wings and diving into the water on a fine day, cocks crowing late at night, and hens rolling in the dust foretell rain. Surprisingly enough, by observing my own poultry, I found the above to be true. It is a sure sign of rain the following day when pigeons are late returning home; but the weather will be mild after day-break if an owl can be heard crying at night. Sparrows chittering loudly and flocking together foretell a storm brewing.

My second grandmother, being a born and bred country person, knows of many superstitions connected with the weather, but there is one in particular that has remained in my mind for many years because when she first told it to me as a child I found it most amusing, and I still do!

> When November's ice is strong enough
> to bear the weight of a duck,
> The winter will be nothing more than
> mud and bloody muck!

There are so many ways to forecast the weather, some are acceptable, others are too absurd to be true. However, there must be some truth in these 'old wives' tales' as they have stood the test of time.

Events that Forecast Rain

When a lot of soot falls down the chimney; when the smoke from the fire blows out of the chimney sideways; if a flame in an oil lamp burns brighter than usual; when household smells become stronger than usual; if glass, iron, marble or salt becomes moist; if the wood of windows and doors begins to smell damp; when corns on the feet become extremely painful!

Bees making short trips from their hive during the day, then returning back in swarms before night fall without being heavily laden with nectar, is a sign of light drizzle. Toads leaping out of their holes in large numbers, moles throwing up a lot of earth, frogs croaking loudly at night, worms appearing on the surface of the soil, are all signs that foretell very heavy rain. When turkeys and cows collect together, when cattle stand or lie down together, sheep eating vast amounts of grass, foretell that rain is near.

Although the following superstition is of American origin, when I stumbled across it, I found it so unusual I had no choice but to include it.

The Animal after which a Day is Named

The American marmot or woodchurck, better known as the ground hog, is considered a weather prophet. American tradition has it that on the second day of February the ground hog comes out of its den for the first time in the year. If the sun is shining and the animal sees its own shadow, it will retreat under ground for another six weeks of slumber. Accordingly, the forecast is continued cold and a late spring. If the day is cloudy and the ground hog fails to see its shadow, it is a sign that the cold weather is over and there will be an early spring. The source of the superstition of Ground Hog Day is not known. It is generally supposed to have originated among the black people of the middle-eastern states, but the legend of Ground Hog Day is actually a remarkable example of the transfer of Old World folklore to the New World. In Europe the second of February is associated with Candlemas Day, but in this instance the hedgehog and the badger play the role of the weather prophet.[6]

'A Saturday's moon comes it once in seven years, . . . comes too soon.' A new moon on Monday is very fortunate. If the moon comes in and goes out on a Sunday, we can only expect the worst of weather. If you point at the moon rain will surely come. When the moon lies on her back in her first quarter, she is holding up all the rain in her lazy curve, but it won't be long before she straightens herself up, pouring the lot down on to us as she does so! It seems that Diana the Moon Goddess foretells nothing except rain.

If a lead-coloured ring can be seen around the moon then rain is promised. If the ring is red, rain and wind can be expected. If the ring is small, light drizzle. If the ring is large, very heavy rain. If there is no ring at all we can only hope and pray for fine weather.

After a beautiful day, when the sun starts to set, if a dark cloud covers the sun, and all that can be seen from behind the cloud are what can only be described as 'fingers of light' pointing outwards in every direction surrounded by the sun's rays shining out brightly from behind the cloud, this is a sure sign of rain the following day. My grandmother has only ever witnessed this spectacular event once in her lifetime. I hope that one day I shall be fortunate enough to do so.

If it rains on St Swithin's Day (July 15th), it is supposed to rain for six weeks thereafter.

To see a rainbow is indeed a glorious and magical sight. As a child, whenever I saw a rainbow I would run for miles to try and stand beneath it before it faded as I believed that it possessed powers which would grant me anything I asked for. But of course, I never did reach the rainbow, no matter how fast I ran towards it the further away from me it seemed to be. Today when I see a rainbow, I no longer run, I stand

---

[6] 'Encyclopedia of Animal Life' The Greystone Press, New York, 1961.

mesmerized by its beauty and as it fades so do my childhood memories of 'rainbow magic'.

God sent a rainbow when Noah reached land after the flood. 'I do set my bow in the cloud, and it shall be for a token of a covenant between me and the earth. And I will remember my covenant, which is between me and you and every living creature of all flesh; and the waters shall no more become a flood to destroy all flesh.' (Genesis, Chapter 9: v13 & 15). To many, the rainbow is a symbol of God's promise that he will never flood the world again; but to me, it's still magic.

My uncle had his own strange way of forecasting the weather. He'd walk for hours on the beach searching for a suitable mass of seaweed. I used to think that he was potty! 'Bubble-weed' I used to call it, as it was covered in hundreds of tiny bubbles, which, to my uncle's disgust, I would spend hours popping. After soaking the seaweed over night in a bucket of cold water, it was then tied together, and nailed to the shed door to dry out. Each day he would check the seaweed before going to work. If it was dry, then it would be warm and sunny. If wet, damp and rain later. If moist, strong winds with rain later during the day.

Events that Forecast Fine Weather

Large numbers of bats flying for a long period of time forecast warm, sunny weather for the following day.

When gnats gather together before sunset into a circling mass; also fine weather when birds fly very high.

Fair weather can be expected when the flames of a fire burn steadily and evenly, and when the smoke goes straight up and out of the chimney.

A sure sign of sunny weather is when the sun sets late in the evening, leaving the sky like a beautiful carpet of red.

Old Saying:

> Red sky at night, Shepherd's delight,
> Red in the morning, Shepherd's warning.

Events that Forecast Rough Weather

A pale yellow sky foretells light wind. Thick heavy white clouds moving quickly across the sky in a storm are a sign of high winds the following day.

When pigs become restless and grunt loudly strong winds are on their way, as pigs are said to be able to see wind!

If the wind changes often and quickly, violent storms are on their way. Strong winds are to be expected if the coals in the grate suddenly actively flare up.

When a cat's tail suddenly stands up straight, windy weather is near. When a female cat turns her back to the fire, a storm is brewing.

Thunder is approaching when cattle draw together then remain still.

Old country folk used to call the poppy 'thunder flower'. It was regarded as an unlucky flower, and they believed that if a young maiden should pick this flower and a stranger should happen to see her, then thunder would descend upon the spot from which she picked the flower. It was also considered an ill omen to pick the poppy, which was known as a flower of death.

Old Saying:

Thunder in Spring, Cold will bring.

Thunder-storms in March or April are followed by a cold May.

Old Weather Wives' Tales

A fog that starts when the weather is mild will last longer than a fog that begins in the wind.

A frost that begins on a windy day will last longer than a frost that begins without a wind.

If a gale calms down at sunset it will increase before midnight; if it calms after midnight then we can expect fine weather the next day.

If the oak comes into bud before the ash it will be a wet summer. When the berries appear early on the holly tree, we can expect a long hard winter.

Old Weather Rhyme:

> If on New Year's night the wind blow South,
> This betokeneth warmth and growth.
> If West, much murk and fish in the sea,
> If North, much cold and snow there will be;
> If East, the trees will bear much fruit.
> But if it be in the North East,
> It is not good for man nor beast. . .!

There will be a grand crop if the sun shines through the apple trees on Christmas Day. And there will be a good hay crop the next year also if there is snow at Christmas. If there is a good wind on Christmas Day the trees will be laden with fruit the following year.

'So far as the sun shines on Christmas Day, so far will the snow blow in May.'

Old Rhyme:

> A warm Christmas, a cold Easter,
> A green Christmas, a white Easter.
> Christmas in snow, Easter in wind,
> A light Christmas, a heavy sheaf.

This section takes me back to the first Christmas I spent in the Cotswolds. Whilst my father was chopping wood for the fire, old Sid the farmer came across to make his acquaintance. While rolling himself a cigarette, he said, 'You'd better chop more wood than that, else you'll all freeze to death. It will be a heavy snow this winter, and a long one at that. The old fox has been barking like a dog all October, sure sign of heavy snow that be.' And old Sid was right, we were snowed in for a week!

5 Wedding Lore

Every village church welcomed a wedding, and weddings in the great houses were indeed festive occasions not only for the family, but for the tenants and the villagers too. Everyone attended. Streamers and garlands decorated the drive gates and the streets on these special occasions. Even the school would close and the children were given a holiday to enjoy the spectacle of triumphal arches stretched across the village streets.[7]

Young future brides-to-be were given motherly advice as to what married life entailed, and how to act appropriately before and after the wedding day to ensure that the course of true love would forever run smoothly. Young maidens were advised to eat a cube of sugar on their wedding eve so that their husbands would always be gentle, loving and kind for many years to come after the happy day. When my grandmother was young, her mother told her that a girl who can build a fire quickly will make a good wife. A man who can achieve this will make a faithful and good husband.

There are endless superstitions connected with weddings, and looking back through the centuries it is hardly surprising!

Wedding Superstitions

Three candles burning at the same time in the same room signify that there will be a wedding in the house fairly soon. There will be no wedding whilst peacock feathers decorate any part of the house. The reason for this superstition could be because the eye that can be seen on the end of the feather is known as the eye of loneliness, but this only applies when a single feather is used for decoration.

---

[7] 'Social Life in Gloucestershire Villages 1850–1950', Glos. W.I. Records

It is very unlucky for the groom to see his bride in her wedding dress until she sails towards him at the altar. The bride should never see herself in her wedding dress by candle light. Should a girl sew a stitch in her own wedding dress or help to make her own wedding cake, her married life will be a life of hard work. Never mark the wedding linen with the first initial of your future husband for you will not bear his name for long. It is best to wait and mark it after the marriage.

It is a sign of good luck for the bride and groom if the family cat sneezes on the wedding day. It is extremely lucky for a chimney sweep to be present at any wedding; better still, if he is family. Lucky is the bride who finds a spider on her wedding dress – she will be rich as well as happy and loved.

A man who is looking for a wife will wear a signet ring on his first finger. If he is engaged, on his second finger; if married on his third or wedding-ring finger. If a man never wishes to marry, he wears the ring on his little finger.

The third finger of the left hand which the engagement and wedding ring is placed on is also significant. The custom to wear the engagement ring on this finger is from an old Roman belief that an artery went straight to the heart from this finger. However, this isn't merely superstition, an artery does lead to the heart from this finger, but then again each finger has an artery that leads to the heart. According to legend, the ring is placed on this finger to ensure that the receiver of the ring will always have love in her heart; but this isn't always so, especially if the ring isn't given with love from the heart, or if the ring is one which has been passed down through the family, which is an old tradition but also a fatal one. If the ring has been worn without love at one stage or another, even though it is given to a new bride as a symbol of love, the marriage will not last long. It is unlucky for a girl to try on her wedding ring before marriage.

It is also very unlucky for the bridegroom to drop the ring at the altar. Many women today wear two wedding rings, the second ring is usually worn on the right hand and once belonged to their mother or grandmother. But superstition has it if an unmarried woman wears a wedding ring on any finger, especially the third finger of the left hand, she will never marry. Anyone who knows me will confirm that I love rings, and I wear a gold wedding ring which belonged to my mother. As I don't particularly adhere to this superstition, I have been known to wear it on my left hand. When my grandma Jess sees the ring on my finger, she goes mad saying, 'Selena you will never marry'. And that's fine by me!

It is said that a good, faithful wife will never remove her wedding ring from her finger. However, if by accident the ring should fall from the finger, no ill-hap need be feared if the husband puts the ring back onto his wife's finger himself. He must say the following as he does so:

> That I bless the day when I first met you,
> And I love you now as I did then,
> Oceans deep, and mountains high.

A stye is a small swelling on the rim of the eyelid. An infallible cure is to rub the stye three times with a gold wedding ring. A gold wedding ring can also be used to tell the sex of an unborn child. Pass a silk thread through the ring and hold it over the expecting mother's stomach; if the ring spins, the child will be a girl, if the ring remains still, then it will be a boy. I've seen this done many times, and it has always turned out to be correct.

Ask a question Run a new silk thread through a gold wedding ring and hold it slightly above a basin of water. Ask one question that can be answered by 'yes' or 'no'. Hold the thread straight and tight when asking the question. If the ring strikes the basin once, the answer is 'no'; if twice, doubtful; if three times, the answer is a clear 'yes'.

When the marriage vows are being said, the one who answers in the loudest voice will have little say in the running of the household.

A bald-headed man at the altar is very unlucky whether he is the minister or the father of the bride. If the married couple turn away from the altar after the ceremony in different directions, separation is on the cards. Both the bride and the groom should try to catch sight of a dark-haired man when they turn from the altar; to see a fair-haired man or woman is unlucky. If the bride and groom leave the church by the same door as the one by which they entered they will be happy in their new life together.

No wedding in the small village of Fingest is supposed to be lucky unless the bridegroom lifts his bride over the church gate when leaving after the ceremony. The gate is locked so that the newly-wed couple cannot get through it. All their relations and friends gather to watch the custom being duly observed.[8]

Roping the bridal carriage as it leaves the church is an old traditional forest custom at weddings which was still carried out in the small village of Coleford up until about fifty years ago. After the marriage ceremony the newly-wed couple were held up in the air on four thick ropes until coins were thrown and scrambled for by onlookers and the awaiting crowd.

An old country custom is for the groom to carry his bride over the lych gate. Another well known wedding custom is for both the bride and groom to hold hands and jump over the church gate whilst the confetti is being thrown. Another wedding tradition, which is still very much alive today, is for the groom to 'pay his way'. After the ceremony, the church gates are locked and children gather around to scramble coins which are thrown by the groom and the best man, then the gates are opened to allow the happy couple through. This particular custom is still carried out in my own village, which accounts for my sister's enthusiasm for weddings!

Today we throw confetti over the newly-weds but originally it was rice. Whether the custom of throwing rice is descended from our forefathers, or more directly from the Roman form of marriage (confarreatio), there is no doubt that the rice is a symbolic expression of hope, purity and fertility. Rice enters largely into the marriage ceremonies of the Far East, being scattered over the heads of the bride and groom whilst the sacred marriage vows are being said. Afterwards the Priest throws rice over the married couple and offers them prayers, asking the Gods to bless them with many healthy strong sons and daughters.

To throw corn at a newly-wed couple is an ancient country

---

[8] *Fingest Church Guide Book*, 1956.

custom. The corn signified faithfulness and ensured both prosperity and fertility in the marriage. This custom is still alive today. In some parts of the small remote villages in Sussex, ears of wheat are thrown at the bride and groom as they pass through the lych gate or the wedding arch.

Like rice and corn, straw has always been connected with fertility rites. An old country custom to ensure fertility was to give the bride-to-be a garter made from straw. The garter, which was worn underneath the going-away dress, was made from the last sheaf, usually by the bride's mother or grandmother. Only a virgin was permitted to wear such a garter; if the bride was not a virgin, the fertility Goddess would revenge the young woman by making her barren as punishment for abusing the gift of fertility. This is now replaced by the modern blue garter which most brides wear today underneath the wedding dress. An old, old rhyme says that the bride should wear something else with her going away dress.

Old Rhyme:

Something old, something new, something borrowed,
Something blue;
And see that the church is full to the chin
Ere ever you let the bride come in. . .

Throwing the wedding bouquet is indeed a very old wedding custom, one which has been carried out for centuries. 'Three times a bridesmaid never a bride!' So the old saying tells us, but if the bridesmaid catches the bouquet for the third time, then there is a chance that she will marry, but not until her latter days, and her chances of marrying a single man are few and far between. It is considered unlucky to catch a bouquet from a bride who has been married twice, each time in white. Unhappy is a married woman if she catches the bride's bouquet.

The common myrtle, (*Myrtus Communis*) was regarded as the 'love flower' and was always connected with Aphrodite, the Greek Goddess of Love. Many myrtles have sprung up from the sprig that Queen Victoria carried in her wedding bouquet. To this day, all Royal brides include myrtle in their wedding bouquets.

Today the honeymoon signifies the month after the marriage, and most of that month is spent away from home. The word 'honeymoon' is so called from the ancient custom that was carried out by the natives from the Northern nations of Europe. After the marriage ceremony the newly-married couple would drink mead, which is a kind of wine made from fermented honey and water with spices added. This would be drunk by the bride, groom and all friends and relations for thirty days after the marriage; hence the name 'honeymonth' or as we know it today, 'honeymoon'. It has been said that Attila the Hun drank so much mead at his wedding feast that it killed him!

The *Evesham Journal* of June 27th, 1863, relates how the Curate of Mickleton returned with his bride from their honeymoon. 'Across the entrance to the village were hung evergreens and garlands; the Union Jack was flying and there was a peal of bells. There was another large arch at the vicarage gates, and another at the entrance door. Fourteen fair young ladies with wreaths on their heads and carrying baskets of flowers strewed the path.'

Although today many women would regard it as romantic to re-marry the same man the second or third time around in the same church as they did the first time, it is said to entice bad luck. For some unknown reason beyond my knowledge, Saturday is considered to be the unluckiest day for a wedding. However, over the years judging by friends and relations, Saturday appears to be the most popular day of the week for a wedding. I expect the main reason for this is because Saturday is the most convenient day for the vicar and working couples. But no vicar will marry anyone if Christmas Day falls on a Saturday. As weddings are somewhat costly nowadays to say the least, I am sure that all fathers and future fathers to be would most certainly welcome back the ancient marriage ceremony of 'Jumping the Broom' which was quick, simple, and cost no more than a brass farthing!

WEDDING ANNIVERSARIES

Anniversary	*Traditional Gifts*
First	Paper
Second	Cotton
Third	Leather
Fourth	Fruit/flowers
Fifth	Wooden
Sixth	Sugar/Sweets/Iron
Seventh	Wool or Copper
Eighth	Bronze or Pottery
Ninth	Willow or Pottery
Tenth	Tin/Aluminium
Eleventh	Steel
Twelfth	Silk/Linen
Thirteenth	Lace
Fourteenth	Ivory
Fifteenth	Crystal
Twentieth	China
Twenty-Fifth	Silver
Thirtieth	Pearl
Thirty-Fifth	Coral
Fortieth	Ruby
Forty-Fifth	Sapphire
Fiftieth	Golden
Fifty-Fifth	Emerald
Sixtieth	Diamond

6 Witchcraft and Legends

Picking up from where I left off, talking of brooms brings me on to my next section – Witches. An ancient superstition proclaims that witches were able to change themselves into hares by saying the following lines three times: 'I shall go into a hare and I shall take its form, I shall go into a hare in the Devil's name.' This enabled the witch to roam the country-side at night without being seen. Once the witch had carried out her evil tasks she would then change back to her usual form, but as her broomstick was not at hand she had no means of transportation, therefore she would gather some ragwort, which was one of her many favourite herbs, and turn it into a horse so that she could quickly fly home over the country-side, as she did not dare take the risk of being seen after sunrise. A bundle of hay would serve if ragwort was not at hand, but she had to work hard at it!

Indeed, the witch had a lot to live up to. It seemed that each village had its own witch, and each witch had her own herbs. However, most were just wise old women who lived alone, were knowledgeable, knew the healing properties of herbs and put them to good use. But alas, their natural earthly cures backfired on them and it was pure ignorance on the part of simple country folk that caused so many innocent lives to be taken.

In the 17th century, a man called Matthew Hopkins became the first 'Witch Finder General' in England. Matthew Hopkins used the method of searching for marks of the Devil on the witch's body. Any scar, birthmark or even an insect bite would convince him that she was a witch. But the witch finder's favourite method was the 'Witch Ducking' or 'Swimming'. Some say that Matthew Hopkins himself died from a 'swimming' in the local pond![9]

The victims were tied hand to foot crosswise, put into a sack, then thrown into the nearest pond or river. All this after having been cruelly tortured and left chained up in some old damp barn awaiting their trial. And their trial was by no means a fair one. Once thrown into the water, if the convicted floated to the surface or by chance managed to swim to the side of the river bank they were found guilty of the crime of witchcraft. They would then either be sentenced to death by the torch or sent to the hanging tree. If they sank and drowned, which many of them did, their name would be cleared and their soul would go to Heaven. The bodies of the innocent were dragged from the muddy river bed, and what was left of them was buried in unhallowed ground, usually in a field behind the church. The villagers still feared them when they were dead; an aspen was laid on the graves to prevent them from rising up and flying abroad.

Many of the witch trials in England and Scotland have been recorded. One of the most famous is that of the witches of Pendle Forest in Lancashire. This was held on August 17th, 1612. It was the first English trial of a large group of witches. There were twenty of them. Fortunately, none were executed, but four were sent to Fleet Prison in London. Another famous trial took place in 1664 at St Edmundsbury. Amy Duny and Rose Cullender were found guilty of witchcraft and hanged at Cambridge.

The last witch to be condemned to death in England was Jane Wenham, in 1712. She was sentenced to die by the judge, but then pardoned after her trial. In the 18th century it all came to an end. In 1736, a new law was made in England to replace the 'Witchcraft Act' that James I had brought in, nearly two hundred years earlier. It said that witches could no longer be punished by death. A person suspected of witchcraft was to be kept in prison for a year and put in the stocks every three months.[10]

As I watch my mother from the window, making her way around the garden with a wooden basket on her arm collecting flowers, berries, and herbs to make home remedies, potions, delightful sweet-smelling pot-pourri and other useful ointments to relieve insect bites, swellings and rashes, I

[9 & 10] *Witches and Wizards* by Elizabeth Cooper, Macdonald, 1978.

dread to think what would happen to her and to me if we were living in the 16th century now. Then a certain hysteria of witchcraft was aroused so much that hardly any married or unmarried woman, young or old, felt safe to be seen out alone during the day or after nightfall. Walking, dancing, picking flowers or attending to crops were indeed believed to be the 'Devil's work' and should rain fall unexpectedly and flood the paddocks the girl was most definitely in communication with the 'Evil One', and would be dealt with according to the law.

Although at first I had my suspicions, I failed to find any solid evidence that there were once witch trials in my own village, even though the surrounding field names – for example, 'Witchie-Pool', 'Hanging Hill' and 'Hanging-Lay' – suggested as much. Even the hunt for a suspected witch was a total loss, at least that was what I thought until I dug deeper and unearthed the well-known but less talked about legend of 'Hetty Pegler'. However, let's leave that aside for now. In the village of Little Compton, better known today as Long Compton, a local witch-hunter claimed that there were sixteen witches in the village; J.A. Brooks covers this accusation further in *Ghosts and Witches of the Cotswolds*. In 1875 James Heywood killed an old lady named Ann Turner or Tennant with a pitchfork at Long Compton. He claimed to be a latter-day witch-hunter and said that Ann Turner was one of the sixteen witches living in the village. By killing her and spilling her blood, he was able to undo the spells she had cast. In court, the crazed young man asked that the body of his victim should be weighed against the Bible, a rare reference to a bizarre and ancient custom.

Legends do, of course, circulate in the village, legends which have been handed down through the generations, although I expect that they have been vastly exaggerated, and no doubt were told by fireside storytellers on many a cold winter's night.

Before I go any further with this next section, I would like to state that although the legends here are listed as just that (with the exception of Helen the Witch), this does not discount the possibility that these events did actually take place.

Also bear in mind the factual evidence on paper or otherwise which cannot be passed off as merely superstition.

LEGENDS

A Haunted Village

Four miles from Cheltenham lies the most haunted village in Gloucestershire. The delightful picturesque village of Prestbury with its looming hills, enchanting olde worlde thatched cottages, narrow streets and winding lanes is an example of a typical Cotswold village steeped in history and literally surrounded by phantoms, ghosts, enchantment and other ghoulish things that go bump in the night. It is this part of Prestbury's history which attracts hundreds of tourists every year.

Prestbury's most famous ghost is that of a 'Cavalier Dispatch Rider' who was ambushed and killed whilst carrying important papers from Sudeley to Gloucester 400 years ago. The old villagers declare the legend of the 'Ghost Cavalier' to be fact, describing how suddenly on the stroke of midnight the silence is broken by the sound of hoofbeats galloping at great speed down Shaw Green Lane, then they gradually fade away into the distance. Throughout the years several residents in the area have been awakened by the sound of hoof-beats, but are somewhat mystified when on investigation they find that there is no visible sign of a horse!

On 'All Souls Eve', a hooded monk with hands crossed and head bowed has been sighted many times walking slowly down the centre aisle of Prestbury church, then making his way past the priory into the main street, where he hesitates slightly before continuing on until finally approaching a landmark called 'Reform Cottage', better known today as the 'Monk's Burial Ground'. After reaching his destination he vanishes. One of the lesser known ghosts of Prestbury is that of an old lady dressed in ancient clothes who peers into the windows of build-

ings in the main street; she disappears by the Almshouses
that were put up by Ann Goodrich in 1720.

A phantom shepherd complete with ghostly sheep
was seen in Swindon Lane on a foggy Autumn night in
1975. Herdsmen have great difficulty in driving their
flocks past the Plough Inn in Mill Street. Dogs also freeze
at this point, their hackles rise and they show the whites
of their eyes – a sure sign of acute distress in a dog.
Horses, too, sense evil here, yet no one can account for it,
unless it has something to do with the apparition known
as Mrs Preece's Ghost, which also haunts Mill Lane. This
has been described as a white misty form which glides
across the fields towards the lane, when it reaches the
wall it seems to hesitate for a moment and then vanishes.

The village of Prestbury is indeed untouched by the modern world and very beautiful. Old thatched cottages, quaint
old mills, inns, tithe barns surrounded by glorious country-
side that appears to be never ending are ideal for city folk to
get away from the fast and noisy hustle and bustle of every-
day life. But I wouldn't advise anyone who has a 'nervous
disposition' to spend their holiday in the delightful haunted
village of Prestbury!

Helen the Witch

A mile or so away from the village school in a small remote
village in the heart of the Cotswolds stands an old oak tree.
In the past this was a very lonely spot and no-one ventured
near it after dark because it was supposed to be haunted by
old Helen the Witch!

To defy superstition, three well known local men slept out
on the grass underneath the tree during the summer. Each
man had a barrel of beer and the celebrations were kept going
just as long as the drink lasted. They spread all kinds of
rumours about a witch and how she walked around the oak
tree twelve times on the stroke of midnight. The majority of
the villagers said that these men could imagine anything after
this amount of beer, but a few people took them seriously, and
really believed all they had said.

This story is centuries old. It has been related that Cromwell and his soldiers one night slept out underneath the tree before going to battle. During the night, they were awakened by the appearance of a witch and they took this to be a bad omen. The following day Cromwell and his Roundheads were completely defeated near Burford. The old oak tree still stands, and even today the villagers prefer to go out of their way rather than near the spot. The legend of old Helen the Witch is what I could call a typical country tale, one which I find most delightful.

Nibley's Ghost

Here is a ghost story that suggests that the ghost, like beauty, is in the eye of the beholder!

Nibley's Ghost haunts the road at the bottom of Stancombe Pitch. On certain nights of the year a ghostly funeral may be seen crossing one of the bridges, with mourners following behind the hearse pulled by six black horses. The driver of the hearse lifts his head from beneath a hooded robe. His face may be the face of an acquaintance – or your own, but whoever's face it is, legend has it that that person will die within a year of the sighting. The trees that made this place very dark have been cut down and for some years there has been no record of the ghost being seen.

The inhabitants of Hargrove House in Cranham were asked by its former owner if they had heard the ghost.

> We had indeed, many times, though we had not known that there was supposed to be one. The ghost has a very natural light, rather busy human footstep, not in the least furtive or frightening, which sometimes is heard in the passage upstairs. Whilst it may be caused by the effect, for example, of contraction or expansion of the oak beams over the old farm kitchen, the effect is so natural that we have often called out to each other or to our small boy – who was fast asleep!

One Hundred Yew Trees

In the 18th century the village of Downham was struck by
smallpox. Small Pox's Hill, also known as 'Corpse Peak'
stands tall in between the two villages of Uley and Cam. At
the back of the peak used to stand Downham Hospital where
the many victims were cared for. One out of every five
families lost loved ones. The bodies of the deceased were put
into a wooden cart which was pulled up the peak by horses.
A large grave was dug and one hundred smallpox victims
were buried there. As it was unhallowed ground one hundred yew trees were planted on the peak to protect the dead
from evil, one tree for each person. Only ninety-nine grew –
the hundreth tree withered and died. Since then, many attempts have been made to make up the hundred but for some
strange reason the last tree would not grow.

Some say that the reason for this was because the tree had
no purpose, as the body lying beneath it was buried alive.
When the tree withered, the person's soul was taken with it
as, according to a strange old superstition the undeparted
soul rightfully belonged to the tree spirit. Many stories have
been handed down through the generations of the ghostly
happenings on the peak. According to one legend, on a
certain night of the year a cart pulled by two pit horses
proceeds up the peak; it is stopped half way up by the Devil
who comes to claim a departing soul due to some agreement
previously made. His penance is to walk unseen amongst the
living dead for all eternity.

Some fifty-five years ago on a warm summer's evening a
young courting couple walked hand in hand around the side
of the peak. As they turned and retraced their tracks, the
gentle breeze suddenly became a strong violent wind, a thick
mist surrounded them and a foul stench filled the air. They
heard the sound of horses' hooves and creaking cart wheels.
This continued for a few minutes, then the mist cleared and
the wind returned calm as though nothing had happened. An
elderly local woman (a friend of my grandmother's) told me
'Down the side of the peak used to be a path which led across
a clearing; it was known to many as Lover's Walk. As it was
quiet and seldom used it was an ideal place for courting

couples to be alone. Harry and I used to enjoy our walks. We had heard of the superstitions but we never took any notice of them, but after that night we never went near the spot again.'

The cart tracks can still be seen today leading up to the top of the peak. Over two centuries have passed but no grass has ever grown over the ancient tracks. To this day each year on Good Friday the local villagers place a cross on the peak, and a service is held in remembrance of the smallpox's victims.

The Ghost Dog

I believe that all animals have souls, and when they pass over in spirit, like humans they retain their earthly form. A dog which has had a loving family will also have happy memories and it's only natural that it would want to return to the house in which it once lived, or to its owners and make its presence known to them. Many people have related their experiences to me and found it a great comfort knowing that their loving, trusting companion had returned to them. I know that I would welcome back my own dog when she has departed from this world, but I'm not sure how I would react if I were staying in someone else's house and during the night was awakened by a dog jumping onto my bed at full force, only to find that there is nothing there!

This has happened several times to family and guests who have stayed in the Ancient Ram Inn. The owner, Mr John Humphries told me: 'Sometimes I can hear a dog scratching at my bedroom door. There is for certain a ghost dog in the Inn; many people apart from myself have seen, felt, or heard it.' Not long after moving into the Inn some twenty-two years ago, his two young daughters were woken by a dog jumping on their bed. They couldn't see anything but they felt four paws walking over them. Where the dog had walked it had left its imprint on the sheet; after a while the dog leapt off the bed and made a loud thud as it hit the wooden floor.

Since then John's eldest daughter has often seen the dog sitting on the stairs with an old shepherd to whom they believe the dog belongs. The dog has been described as a grey and white cross collie. Although the dog makes its presence known, those who have tried to touch it quickly pull their hand away and stand back, as their hand disappears and goes straight through it. Then the dog vanishes before their eyes. One person who has touched the dog told me that he had never before experienced anything like it. 'My hand went right through the dog, I couldn't feel anything, but I knew that it was there because I could see it; afterwards my hand felt cold and numb.'

One young man, whilst staying at the Inn, was first woken during the night by the dog, then on another occasion sighted the dog with the shepherd. On the night of May 31st 1985, while sleeping in the Berkeley Room during the early hours of the morning he was suddenly awakened by something standing on his chest. He could feel four legs and naturally assumed that it was a dog, but when he turned on the light there wasn't anything there. He moved over to the far side of the bed, covering his face with the blankets in sheer fright. He felt the dog jump off the bed, then heard a loud thud on the floor. He sat up in bed and looked around the room, but there was nothing to be seen.

The following day he felt the presence of a dog brush past him on the stairs. At the top of the stairs a stream of light came up through the floorboards. At the same time a wispy grey mist slowly arose which developed into the outline of a man. He shielded his eyes and turned his head away from the blinding light. When the light had completely faded he saw an old man dressed as a shepherd, in human form, not at all ghost-like. The dog was nothing more than a black shadow in the shape of a dog which was lying beside his feet on the floor. After a few minutes the shepherd began to fade backwards into the wall. As it did so, the hazy light which surounded him grew dimmer, the ghost returned to a grey mist, then disappeared into the wall completely. The black shadow of the dog became a black mass which also disappeared into the wall. That evening when he told the owner, he laughed, 'You're not the first to see him, and no doubt not the last!'

The King Stone

In a small village stands a large stone on a high peak which the local folk call 'The King Stone'. According to legend, long ago during the 13th century a Pagan King climbed the peak and shouted out that one day he would become the King of England. A witch who lived nearby, on hearing this, cast him into a large stone and his companions into small ones, which are better known as the Whispering Knights. The Whispering Knights lie two miles from the village of Long Compton. Fifty-eight stones are situated in a circle, one hundred feet in diameter. Many witches dance around these stones, as the Whispering Knights are said to be able to tell the past, present and the future if you possess the power to hear them!

Tradition tells how a King once set out to conquer England, and as he came up the hill from the village of Great Rollright and beheld the grand view over Little Compton, he was halted by a witch who instructed him to take seven long strides and then said:

> If Long Compton thou canst see
> King of England thou shalt be.

The King, elated by thoughts of such an easy victory, cried 'Stick, stock, stone, As King of England I shall be known.' Eagerly, he turned off the road towards the crest of the hill – but after taking seven long strides he found himself faced not by Long Compton but by the long mound of earth. Then said the witch:

> As Long Compton thou canst not see,
> King of England thou shall not be,
> Thou and thy men hoar stones shall be,
> And I shall be a eldern tree.

As the witch pronounced these words the King turned into stone and his army across the road likewise became monoliths. While the witch became an elder tree, the cunning old lady delayed her transformation until she had also made stones of the Whispering Knights, who had lagged behind and were plotting treason.

It has been said that the witch owned the land and didn't take too kindly to intruders, especially the Pagan King who tried to outsmart her, which is why she turned him into stone. The Whispering Knights are better known to many as the Rollright Stones. The long mound of earth which the King was confronted with still remains to this day as does the elder tree. The local saying is 'Never mention a witch for fear of seeing one!'

The Legend of Hetty Pegler's Tump

The legend of Uley Long Barrow, better known as 'Hetty Pegler's Tump' both intrigued and fascinated me right from the beginning. The magic of the tump which is captured in the stone is far from lost but will never be fully revealed. The mystery which surrounds it merely adds to one's curiosity, and arouses the spirit of imagination which dwells within us all. The name of the place where the tump is situated (Uley), when traced back into Hebrew means 'Olah', burnt offerings, a place of lifting up for sacrifice and voice of prayer. The tump is thousands of years old, built roughly in 2800 BC. The position of the tump, being high up on the edge, was symbolic. The egg shaped burial mound represented the womb of the Earth Goddess, and the rite of internment was the inhumation of the unburnt body.

According to legend Hetty's lovers sacrificed themselves to her by entering the main chamber inside the tump which was then sealed off. The tump was completely covered with wood, which must have taken a lot of hard work by whoever wanted the tump to remain secret, as you will see by the following:

Dimensions	120 feet long, 85 feet broad, 10 feet high.
Entrance	Two upright stones supporting a large flat stone 8 feet x 4 1/2 feet.
Interior	Walls of neat dry masonry. Passage down the centre 22 feet long, 4 1/2 feet wide and 5 feet high, faced with large flat stones. Roof formed of flat stones, 3 separate chambers divided by large flat stones.

In all 13 human skeletons were found in the entrance among

stones and rubbish in the chambers, which coincides with the legend above. Boars' jaws, tusks, charcoal, broken earthenware, flints, and two axe heads were also found. Roman coins were also found with a burial near the summit.

The field was covered with a beech wood, which hid the burrow. In 1820 the wood was cut down, and labourers digging for stone broke into the north chamber where they found two skeletons. After a lapse of 34 years the bury was reopened in August 1854. The Rev W.L. Baker, father of Thomas Lloyd Baker of Hardwicke Court, and the Rev Samuel Lysons were present. The author Bigland says that the 'designation is treated by the peasantry with some awe.' But he doesn't explain why! No doubt the peasantry had invented tales of hauntings, curses, etc over the hundreds of years the barrow had stood there.

Who was Hetty Pegler? Was she a witch? The peasantry certainly believed that she was.

An examination of a list of baptisms in the four parishes surrounding the site of Hetty Pegler's Tump reveals that there were six baby girls whose parents were named Pegler, and they were given the Christian name of Hester, as follows:

Place of Birth	Date of Birth
1. Kings Stanley	1671
2. Kings Stanley	1707
3. Nympsfield	1770 Parents Richard and Mary
4. Woodchester	1800 Twin Girls
5. Stonehouse	1651

All six babies were named Hester Pegler, and the name Hester is often converted into Hetty. It seems odd that both of the twin girls were given the same name! It would be very unlikely that a girl from Kings Stanley, Woodchester or Stonehouse would frequently visit this barrow so many miles from her home, but the Nympsfield Hetty Pegler may have done so.

The name Pegler is a very common surname in this area. There are several Peglers buried in my own village, but the relatives of the deceased are not related to any of them, much

to my disappointment. On the chancel wall of Nympsfield
Church is a table recording the deaths of:

A. Henry Pegler, died August 12th 1695 aged 85

B. His wife Hester, who died November 26th 1694 aged 69.

This couple left some land, the proceeds from which were
to be given to the poor of the parish. Perhaps they owned the
ground where the barrow was made, and perhaps the poor
were allowed into the woods to gather kindling; it can only be
conjecture. But the Christian name Hester or Hetty was still
in use in the Pegler family one hundred years later, when
Richard and Mary christened their baby daughter in 1770. It
is recorded that in 1690 a man named Pegler sold some land
to a clothier (i.e. cloth manufacturer) named Small of Nailsworth.
This seems to point to the Henry Pegler who died and was
buried at Nympsfield in 1695.

I found that people were very hesitant to talk about this
legend in particular. In fact, I only had to mention the name
Hetty Pegler and instantly people were uneasy. This alone
told me that there was far more to this than folk wanted me
to believe.

As you can see from the map, the Nympsfield Hetty Pegler
may have visited this ancient barrow frequently, as it would
be very unlikely that a girl from Kings Stanley, Woodchester
or Stonehouse would travel so many miles from her home.

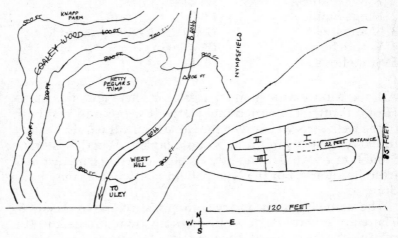

In 1987 a man named Ben Wilson visited Hetty Pegler's Tump and was inspired to sculpt a chair out of wood. He generously gave it to the residents of Uley, which caused great uproar – some of the villagers loved it, others despised it. After many heated discussions, the chair was removed from the village green. The chair, which is a true masterpiece, now stands in a dismal corner in a local art centre.

Shortly afterwards, another event took place. A group of people (including some musicians and poets), danced around the ancient burial ground scattering flowers and chanting a poem based on the history of the tump. Was this performance for paying onlookers, or some kind of significant ritual?

We will never know who the real Hetty Pegler was. Her identity remained a secret for thousands of years and will continue to do so for centuries to come.

Although feared by the peasantry, her lovers supposedly willingly sacrificed themselves to her by entering the main chamber alive. This rules out the possibility of her being a witch, but a Pagan 'High Priestess' is feasible. Her followers respected and honoured her by sacrifically naming every baby girl born into the sect after her. This ceremony of honour was still undertaken one hundred years after the death of the Kings Stanley 'Hetty Pegler'.

The reason for the ritual of naming every baby girl Hetty (or Hester) was to ensure that after the death of one Hetty Pegler the next girl in line of birth would take her place, thus making it impossible for anyone to discover the true identity of the real Hetty Pegler. Many have tried to unravel the mystery and intriguing secrecy of the Hetty Pegler saga, but all have failed . . . including me!

The Three Sisters

Over a loomed hill leading down into a small village, along a narrow street stand three thatched cottages. On a wall is inscribed the date 1720, and the words underneath read, Left to the religious poor by Ann Goodrich. A very uncommon name, but most appropriate. Close at hand, past the cottages on a hill stand three trees, the only ones that can be seen across the vast swept common, standing out like silent sentinels. They attract attention and seem to draw people irresistibly towards them. Through the trees a small house can be seen partly hidden underneath a steep bank, where at one time, long ago lived three beautiful sisters. It is a very sad story and it all happened like this. Each of the sisters had a love affair, and all three were said to be madly in love. What happened nobody rightly knows but each gentleman in turn failed to keep an appointment and was never seen again. Time after time the sisters went to the spot and waited, hoping that their lovers would one day turn up but they never came. All three were broken hearted and vowed they would dedicate the rest of their lives to helping the sick and needy. This they faithfully carried out and no one ever asked for help in vain. Many a sick person owed their life to the constant devotion of one or the other of the three sisters, and their name was loved and respected for miles around. They carried on their good work almost to the last, even when they were unfit for these duties, and never a word of complaint was uttered. Their last wish was to be buried at the spot where they used to wait in vain for their lovers, from where on a clear day quite a number of counties can be seen. In their memory three trees were planted there and named The Three Sisters, Faith, Hope and Charity.

> Like Silent Sentinels:
> Ever on guard they stand
> Over the smiling land,
> Each sentinel a tree –
> Faith, Hope and Charity.
> Faith to make strong,
> Hope like a song,
> Charity for things gone wrong.

Since those days many other trees have been planted there, but for some unaccountable reason no more than three trees would ever grow. The Three Sisters are a landmark for miles around. What better memorial could there be for three sisters who devoted their lives to the good of others and in the darkest hours brought a little sunshine to their less fortunate fellow creatures. How many of us today could make some-one's life a little brighter, thus making the world a happier place to live in? And would we not all feel better for helping someone who has fallen by life's wayside, instead of, as many of us do, turn a blind eye and pass by on the other side of the road like the Levite in the parable of the good Samaritan?

Welcome to the Portcullis

The Portcullis is an historical building full of character and spirit. Built in the year 1650 and situated in the delightful village of Hillsely, it is a welcome place for any traveller wishing to seek food and shelter. The fire is always stocked, the barrels full, the food is exquisite and the atmosphere friendly. The fact that the restaurant is haunted doesn't deter customers. Many people dine at the Portcullis hoping to catch a glimpse of the ghost which is a constant topic of conversation, especially amongst the older villagers.

The ghost is thought to be a monk. A secret passageway runs beneath the restaurant to the Fleece Inn, also in Hillsely, and to 'Monks Mill' an old local landmark a mile or so away from the Portcullis. The passage is also said to lead directly to Kingswood Abbey. As no one has ever removed the slabs that conceal the entrance or ventured inside, there is no real evidence that it does actually lead to the Abbey, but according to the old villagers it does.

Richard and Margaret Pollard who own the Portcullis, knew that it was haunted when they bought it. They have kept an open mind on the subject but Margaret admits that she would be scared if suddenly confronted by the ghost.

The house itself is most welcoming and has a 'nice' feeling about it, not at all eerie in any way. The ghost doesn't bother them or cause them any harm; there have been occasions of what I would call naughty pranks, but never anything disruptive or frightening.

Not long after they had moved in, whilst working in the bar, their dog Dougal suddenly leapt up, his hackles rose and he went absolutely beserk. The dog has done this several times, presumably when the ghost makes his presence known, which is usually about 1.00 am. The previous owners also experienced this and their two dogs would not go down to the lower end of the restaurant where the secret passageway lies beneath.

In 1988, on St Valentine's Day, one of the waitresses went to clear a table in the alcove of the restaurant, the table at which my parents always dine (unfortunately they have never seen the ghost, but the temperature does suddenly drop in the alcove and my mother feels a cold tingling sensation run down her back). There were two candles on the table. One had burnt completely normally, the other had burnt down and the wax had formed itself around the base of the holder into the shape of a hand, as though someone had been holding it while it was burning. Every other candle in the restaurant that night had burnt down normally.

The ghost often plays tricks on them; objects go missing, then reappear, books are moved from one place to another, and the sound of invisible footsteps is often heard. Once Margaret had made fans and placed two in a glass on each table in the restaurant. She left the room and when she returned one fan had been removed from the glass and unfolded. She folded it again, placed it in the glass and left the room. On her return exactly the same thing had happened. After about six attempts she gave up!

On one occasion the ghost played a prank which one can only describe as demonstrative. No one was harmed, they were merely surprised. They were washing glasses in the room behind the bar when they suddenly heard a loud crash. On investigation they discovered that a picture had come off the wall in the bar. It wasn't until later that it dawned on them that the hook and string were still in place so there was no reason for it to fall. The force with which it fell and the damage to the top of the sideboard that stands beneath it and the mere fact that the picture had landed halfway across the room meant that the picture had literally 'flown' off the wall.

There have been sightings of the ghost by customers; it tends to steer clear of the restaurant until closing time. He has been sighted standing by the bar and the fireplace, each time being described as a faint 'body' form.

The Portcullis would most certainly be incomplete without

the ghost who is a legend within his own right which is passed down to children from their parents and will in turn be passed down to future generations for centuries to come. Should you ever dine at The Portcullis and see a figure standing alone drinking a mug of ale, don't scream, assume your imagination is working overtime or your eyes are playing tricks on you. Show him respect, he is very selective; if you do see him you should feel highly honoured!

Witchie Pool

The legend of 'Witchie Pool' is well known and often talked about by the local villagers. It has been handed down through the generations and no doubt slightly exaggerated.

A mile or so away from my cottage, at the back of the old church, is a field which used to be known as 'Potter's Field' or 'Potter's Piece'. Many years ago it was used as a burial ground for strangers. A stone can be seen nearby which was erected in memory of Benj. Clark, a postman. It is this clearing that some of the old local folk call 'Witchie Pool'. The reason is this: long ago a witch is said to have lived there. She spent most of her time sitting by a pool, mixing her magical potions. She lived there for many years without any interference from the villagers, until there was a family feud and the land was divided.

The new farmer wanted her off his land, as the field was good pasture for cattle, and the three surrounding fields were arable land for planting such crops as wheat and barley. The farmer asked her to leave, offering her money. She waved her hands in the air, saying 'Money be of no use to me'. The next day, the farmer returned. He tried reasoning with the witch but she was adamant. 'I'll burn you off my land,' the farmer shouted angrily. 'Ye do that and I'll curse your harvest, it'll burn to dust as I; think farmer, before ye do anything, this be my land, be off with you.'

As she refused to leave, one night (the story goes) the farmer with his men and dogs chased her off the land, beating her with stout sticks. As she ran away she turned in anger and cursed him and his field and then she disappeared and no-one ever saw her again.

Ever since that night nothing has ever grown in that field except weeds, bracken and grass. Witchie Pool is better known today in the village as 'The Old Wreck'. All that remains to be seen on the site is a round hole partly filled with earth which people throw their rubbish into as they pass by.

Spells

I have included this short section on spells purely for interest and fun! If you are looking for a spell to cause anyone any harm then you will be disappointed, and are reading the wrong book.

This is a small collection which I have gathered together over the years from family and friends; many are merely harmless games which young girls practised out of interest, sheer fascination, and with much delight to determine whether they would marry, whom they would marry, and to discover what kind of man their future husband would be.

In my grandmother's days, these so-called spells were taken seriously, and were performed in secret. The fact that they knew that they would be severely punished for their wrong doing if found out, merely added to the excitement and mystery of it all.

I am a great believer in both the magical and healing properties of herbs, which many of the spells in the first section consist of. I frequently use several of them, and they *do* work. For centuries herbs have been associated with magic and witchcraft. The superstitions connected with herbs are both intriguing and fascinating. This certain aura of magic which surrounds herbs and plants alike has always attracted me, which is why I have combined the two together throughout the book. At the end of the day what it comes down to is belief; if, for example, you perform the 'feather spell' (which was successful for a friend of mine) and you acquire what you asked for, you would no doubt class it as a spell. Whatever spell you are looking for I'm sure that you will find one here to suit your needs. With luck, belief, and a touch of magic, anything is possible!

SPELLS FOR ALL AILMENTS
ACHES AND PAINS

Arnica

Tincture of arnica is particularly helpful to ease the pain of sprains and bruises. Apply to the affected area with a piece of lint or cotton wool. For a bad sprain, soak a strip of lint, muslin or cotton wool in the arnica, wrap around the ankle or wrist, then secure in place with a warm bandage. Repeat this every 1–2 hours. The same applies for bruises.

Basil Infusion

For the relief of nausea and vomiting. This can also be taken as a remedy for indigestion. Pick a small handful of young fresh basil leaves; place in a warm tea pot and cover with boiling water. Allow to stand for 5–10 minutes. Take a small cupful every 1–2 hours. When repeating this, use fresh leaves each time.

Comfrey Ligament

For relief of bruises, swellings and sprains. Gather a large handful of fresh comfrey leaves, put into a china cup, earthenware or glass jug (never use a plastic container), cover with half a pint of boiling water; cover with a lid and allow to steep until the water has cooled. Strain. Either apply to the affected area with a piece of lint, muslin or cotton wool; or soak a strip of lint in the infusion, wrap around the knee, ankle or wrist, secure with a warm bandage. Repeat every 1–2 hours.

Comfrey Ointment

For insect bites, cuts and grazes.

You Will Need
1 handful of fresh comfrey leaves
8 ounces of vaseline

Put the vaseline in a bowl standing in a saucepan of boiling water. Add the chopped comfrey. Simmer over a low heat for 20 minutes. Remove bowl of melted vaseline and comfrey, strain through a sieve lined with muslin. Pour into a jar. Keep in the fridge until needed.

Garlic Ointment

To ease sprains and muscular pain.

You Will Need
8 ounce jar of vaseline
2 garlic cloves

Melt the vaseline, using the same method as above. Crush the garlic cloves very finely using a pestle and mortar, or you could use a bowl and the back of a wooden spoon. Add the crushed garlic to the vaseline, then melt together. Remove from heat after 20 minutes; pour into a jar. Place in the fridge until needed.

Marigold Ointment

For bites, swellings and heat rashes.

You Will Need
1 small jar of vaseline
1–2 cupfuls of fresh orange coloured marigold petals.

Put the marigold petals in an earthenware jug and completely cover the petals with boiling water. Cover with a lid, allow to stand for 25 minutes. Strain, and add the infusion to the vaseline. Simmer over a low heat for 20 minutes. Strain through a sieve lined with muslin. Store in a jar in the fridge until needed.

Rosemary Rub

To ease cramps in the stomach rub gently with a mixture of 2 tablespoons of pure sunflower oil and 2–3 drops of oil of rosemary.

To Cure Cramp

To relieve night-time cramp of the lower limbs. Sew a few corks into a small cotton square pillow and pin this to the inside of the bed sheets. When the cramp has stopped the pillow must be burnt.

Charm

A potato, when carried in the pocket, will keep rheumatism at bay. (My grandfather Jubal swore by this and carried a potato in his trouser pocket all his life.)

Nose Bleeds

To stop a nose bleed, place a rolled up yarrow leaf inside the nose. Remove once the bleeding has stopped. Or place a cold flat door key on the back; which will stop a slight nose bleed.

Wart Spell

To cure warts, rub daily with the milky white fluid from the stem of a freshly picked dandelion. This really does work, as I have used this myself. The fluid will stain the skin a light brown colour. After applying, do not wash the hands. Eventually the wart will decrease in size, and fall off.

Wart Spell

Take a fine pin and prick the wart; then stick the pin into a piece of meat and bury it deep in the ground. As the meat rots, your wart will gradually disappear!

SPELLS TO CURE ALL AILMENTS
EYES

Borage Eye Lotion for Sore Eyes

Pick a handful of borage flowers, leaves and stems. Steep in a china cup or earthenware jug, covered with boiling water for 25 minutes. Then strain. When cool, soak two round pieces of lint in the infusion, then place over the eyes. Sit in a darkened room with you head tilted backwards for 10–15 minutes.

Elder Flower Lotion for Tired Puffy Eyes

Pick a handful of fresh elder flowers; remove any marked petals. Steep in an earthenware jug covered with boiling water. Allow to infuse for 30 minutes. Strain and bottle. Bathe eyes morning and night with a piece of lint or cotton wool to reduce puffiness around the eyes.

Fennel Eye Bath

Fennel is excellent for the eyes. It will help swellings, styes and will cure infection, in animals as well as humans. Many swear by fennel tea, saying that it will absorb poisons in the body. Pick a handful of the herb and allow to steep in the usual manner until the water has cooled. Then strain. Bathe the eyes with the infusion as often as required.

Rosewater Eye Bath

You Will Need
5 ml spoonful boric acid powder
½ pint water, boiled
1 tablespoon of rosewater

Dissolve the acid powder in the water. Add the rosewater. Pour into a clean bottle, shaking well. Use daily to refresh the eyes.

Rose Lotion for Sore Strained Eyes

Pick a large handful of white rose petals (Rosaceae), disregarding any marked petals. Place in an earthenware jug and pour over the boiling water enough to completely cover the petals. Cover with a lid and allow to stand for 30 minutes. Strain and bottle when cool. Apply with a clean piece of lint.

To Improve Your Eyesight

If you possess an emerald ring, gaze deep into the stone, then close your eyes and hold the vision of the colour green in your mind's eye. This is said to improve the eyesight if done regularly. If your eyesight is good, this method can be reversed to help someone else. Sit opposite the person, gaze into the ring then look directly into their eyes, transferring the colour green by thought. Or alternatively, place an emerald ring in a glass containing pure mineral water. Take this outside and place in direct sunlight for 2–3 hours. Remove the ring, and use the water to bathe the eyes daily.

The Whites of the Eyes

The whites of the eyes should be clear. Any sign of redness means strain on the eyes, and maybe a slight cold in the eyes. A yellow tinge in the eyes is a sign of the 'liver'. To remove a yellow tinge in the eyes, drink a glass of water with the juice of one fresh lemon added each morning instead of a cup of tea or coffee.

For bright eyes, eat a fresh sprig of parsley three times a day. An old superstition says, 'If you wear a freshly-opened dandelion every day behind the right ear, you will never have cause to wear glasses'.

SPELLS FOR COLDS AND HEADACHES

Elder Rob

This is my favourite health drink. I drink it cold from the fridge in the summer, and hot during the winter to prevent colds. This recipe dates back to 1773. Elder rob is full of vitamin C, and has a curative power of great repute. As a remedy, it is taken hot at night to promote perspiration in the early stages of severe colds, and for symptoms such as shivering and sore throats. It is also taken for influenza, asthma and chest complaints. It is an excellent all-round tonic that I highly recommend.

You Will Need
5 lb of fresh elder berries
1 lb of white sugar

Put the berries into a large saucepan, add a tablespoon of cold water and then stir in the sugar. Simmer on a low heat until it is as thick as honey, stirring every few minutes. Remove from the heat and strain through a sieve using a wooden spoon to mash the berries. Sieve two or three times, then allow to cool. Bottle and store. Lasts up to 8 months.

To drink in the summer, add 2 tablespoons to a glass of water. I use bottled spring water.

To drink in the winter, add 2 tablespoons to a glass of hot water. If you are taking it for a cold, add a few drops of brandy, or, to sweeten, add a pinch of ground cloves or ground cinnamon.

This can also be used as a gargle for a sore throat, or as a cough remedy.

Garlic Cold Cure

To bring relief of severe colds

You Will Need
2 cloves of crushed garlic
Juice of 1 fresh lemon
1 tablespoon of sweet honey
½ teaspoon of ginger
Pinch of cayenne pepper
1 cup of boiling water

Put all the ingredients into a china cup and pour over the boiling water. Cover with a saucer and leave to infuse for 10 minutes. Strain through a sieve. Drink while hot.

Honey and Lemon

This is a delightful drink to help in the early stages of a cold, and to help soothe a sore throat.

You Will Need
1 tablespoon of sweet honey
Juice of half a lemon
A pinch of ground cloves
(Enough for one person)

Put the honey into a glass or china cup. Pour boiling water over, add the lemon juice and ground cloves, stir well. Drink whilst hot. Not only is this pleasant to drink, it's quick to make and simple!

Lemon Balm

This soothing, pleasant drink will help a cold, ease a sore throat, and induce relaxation.

1 teaspoon of lemon balm leaves per cup, enough for one person, and 1 teaspoon for the pot. Place the leaves, whole or freshly chopped in a warm but dry teapot. Pour boiling water over the leaves, and allow to stand for 3–5 minutes. Then strain. Serve with a slice of lemon and a teaspoon of honey. Take as often as required.

Sage for Congestion of the Nose and Head

As sage is a potent herb, use one teaspoon to half a pint of water, two teaspoons to a pint, etc. Sage is excellent as an inhalation for congestion of the nose and head. Steep the leaves in boiling water for 3–5 minutes, then strain. Add the infusion to a basin of boiling hot water. Cover your head with a towel and inhale.

Take a cupful of the infusion morning and night for a cold. Use cold as a gargle to ease a sore throat or an ulcerated mouth.

Rosemary Chest Rub

Apply to the chest to help relieve the sinuses and ease nasal congestion. Do not use if the skin is broken, sore or sensitive.

You Will Need
1 small jar of vaseline
1 handful of rosemary flowers and leaves
8 drops of oil of rosemary

Steep the rosemary flowers and leaves in an earthenware jug covered with boiling water for 20–25 minutes. Then strain. Melt the vaseline in a bowl standing in a saucepan of boiling water. Add the rosemary infusion and simmer on a low heat for 20 minutes, stirring well. Remove from heat, allow to cool, then add the oil of rosemary and stir well. Unlike the other ointments, do not store in the fridge. Stir well before applying to the chest.

To Clear a Head Cold

You Will Need
4 drops of oil of cloves
4 drops of oil of lavender
3 drops of oil of peppermint
5 drops of oil of rosemary

Mix all the oils together in a glass container as listed above. Shake well. Either carry this with you and inhale directly from the bottle, or sprinkle a few drops onto a hanky and inhale. To relieve congestion during the night, sprinkle a few drops onto your pillow, so that you will inhale the oil as you sleep. When not in use, store in a dark place away from sunlight, as oils tend to evaporate within a few months.

Headache Cure

To bring relief to a headache, apply a little eau-de-cologne to the forehead, sit in a darkened room with a warm hanky soaked in water wrung out and applied to the head.

Vinegar Pack

Soak a large hanky in half a pint of hot water (not boiling) to which 3 tablespoons of vinegar have been added. Fold the hanky 3 or 4 times, wring out. Apply to the forehead. Sit in a darkened room with your head tilted backwards to avoid drips in the eyes. Repeat when necessary to aid relief.

Lavender Tonic

For the treatment of headaches and fainting. Make a standard brew of freshly picked or dried lavender flowers; strain. Take a small cupful morning and night. The flowers can be added to other teas with advantage. When drinking lavender tea by itself do not add honey or lemon to sweeten. (Do not take if you have low blood pressure.)

Marjoram Pack

To relieve a cough and ease a sore throat. Make a strong brew of marjoram and soak a cotton cloth in the infusion. Wring out, fold, and bind around the throat whilst hot. At the same time, to treat a headache, drink as a tea. 1 large teaspoon of marjoram to half a pint of boiling water, allow to stand for 5–8 minutes; strain. Drink freely, honey can be added. Or add a few sprigs to a bowl of hot soup.

Mint Cold Pack

To ease a throbbing headache. Pick a handful of mint leaves. Put the leaves into an earthenware jug, pour over half a pint of boiling water. Allow to steep for 5–6 minutes. Strain. Soak a hanky in the infusion until the water turns cold. Fold the hanky, wring out, apply to the forehead. Sit in a darkened room. Repeat if necessary.

Mint and Potato Cold Pack

This is a stronger treatment to relieve a headache, and a rather funny one.

You Will Need
1 small potato
1 pint of boiling water
2 large handfuls of fresh mint leaves
1 large cotton hanky
A tea-cloth

Steep the mint leaves in a jug covered with boiling water. Allow to infuse for 10–15 minutes. Then strain and leave to cool. When cold, steep the slices of raw peeled potato in the mint infusion for 10 minutes. Apply 2–3 slices to the forehead, placing a hanky wrung out in the water over them. Then place over this a dry tea-cloth and tie to keep them all in place. Change the potato slices with freshly steeped ones at regular intervals.

Mint and Vinegar Cold Pack

Steep a handful of mint leaves in half a pint of apple vinegar overnight. Strain through a sieve, soak a cotton cloth of hanky in the cold mint vinegar lotion for 10–15 minutes then wring out and apply to the forehead. Renew frequently. This is an excellent headache remedy.

DREAM SPELLS

I Dream To See

This spell must only be done on St Luke's Day (October 11th).

You Will Need
1 handful of marigold flowers
A sprig of marjoram
A sprig of thyme
A little wormwood
2 tablespoons of virgin honey (clear honey)
A few drops of vinegar

Dry all the herbs before an open fire. Rub them together with your fingers to crumble, then crush to a fine powder in a bowl using the back of a wooden spoon, then sieve. Simmer this over a low heat, adding the honey and vinegar. Anoint yourself with this before going to bed, then say the spell 3 times:

> St Luke, St Luke be kind to me,
> In dreams let me my true love see.

To See a Vision

This is a very old country spell to bring a vision of your future husband. Pick an ounce of St John's Wort and a handful of fresh Rosemary at sunrise. Allow to dry a little before sewing into a small muslin bag. Place this underneath your pillow while repeating the spell:

> St John I pray have pity,
> In a vision let me see my future
> Husband to be.
> Scent of Rosemary, open hearts,
> Let me, my true love never part.

Dream Spell

On the Eve of Midsummer (June 23rd) go out secretly at midnight and pick a ripe red rose (the stronger the scent the better). Set alight a dish containing charcoal and sulphur of brimstone, hold the rose over the burning dish for 5–10 minutes. Then wrap the rose in a sheet of plain white paper on which you have written your own name and the name of your lover. Fold the paper once and seal it with the wax of a red candle. Take the packet outside and bury it underneath the same bush from which you picked the rose. It must remain buried there until the eve of July 6th. On the eve, dig up the packet and place it under your pillow and say the spell as you do so:

> In my dreams I wish to see
> The man that is to marry me.

Speak to no one before picking the rose. Your dreams shall tell you many things about your lover or future husband to be. If you find your dream hard to understand, or should you want to know more, go out again the following year on June 23rd at midnight and secretly pick another rose from the same bush, place underneath your pillow and say the spell. If after the first night you do not dream, the spell can be done a second time, then once more. If after 3 times you do not dream or see your lover in your dreams then you are never to marry. (The above must be done before placing the rose underneath the pillow.)

Dream Spell

On the last night of the year take nine keys. The keys must be either begged or bought, never borrowed. Plait your hair with three ribbons and tie the keys to the end of the plait. Once you have laid down to sleep say the spell:

> Kind St Peter be not amiss,
> To win your favour, I do this,
> You are the ruler of the keys,
> Favour me now if you please;
> Let me your strong influence prove,
> And see my dear and wedded love. . .

If you do not see your future husband in your dream that night, the spell can be done again, but not with the same nine keys, and it can only be carried out on the last night of the year. When repeating this spell for the second time, put a pair of shoes at the foot of your bed in the shape of a T, then say the following:

> Kind St Peter, I dream to see,
> So I place my shoes into a T. . .

Is Your Lover Faithful?

Take a hanky from your lover bearing his initials. Sprinkle a little powdered rosemary onto it then roll it up and tie with three ribbons. Place this under your pillow. If when you awake the ribbons are still tied as you left them, sincere he may be, but his feelings are not true. If knotted and tight, his love is strong and steadfast; if loose, affection he is seeking elsewhere!

To Bring Visions of your Future Spouse

There are several things that when placed underneath a pillow are supposed to bring the sleeper a vision of his or her future spouse. There are so many the list is endless. Here are just a few:

A four-leaved clover
A sprig of rosemary
Heather
Honeysuckle
Lavender
A piece of wedding cake wrapped in a white silk hanky
A flower from a bride's bouquet
Confetti or a piece of lace from a bride's wedding dress
A lock of your lover's hair
A toad!

SPELLS FOR GOOD FORTUNE

A Spell for Fortune

Like the hazel, the ash tree has always been regarded as a very magical tree. It is said that its roots and branches bind Earth, Heaven and Hell together. When you fall upon hard times, stand beneath the tree with your back facing the moon. Repeat the spell 3 times:

> Ashen tree, Ashen tree,
> Pray bring good fortune unto me. . .

To Bless a Child

To bless a child with luck, fortune and to ensure good health, rub the child's heels with a silver coin. The coin must then be kept, never lost or spent. As long as the coin is kept its power shall remain. If the coin is lost, the child in later life will suffer dire misfortune, and will never be lucky in love or successful in business. If the coin is spent, the child will suffer great illness. The child's hands may also be rubbed to bless the child with kindness and talent.

A Spell for Success

This spell is for anything and everything. For a successful business, money, the house of your dreams, or success in love. It will bring instant success in whatever you ask of it!

By the light of the moon wrap a light blue feather in a new unused five pound note, asking what you want as you wrap the feather. Wear this close to your heart if you asked for love. Carry it in your purse if you asked for money. If business, keep in an account book. If a child, move of house, travel, or something to do with a change, bury it in hallowed ground towards the west. Once you have received what you asked for the feather must be given to someone else, and the money must be spent.

It has been said that the singer Madonna used to carry a blue feather wrapped in a five-pound note everywhere she went, but whether it's true is beyond me. Four years ago a friend came to me and asked for a spell to bring love into her life. I gave her a list, many of the items on which are mentioned in this section, and she chose this one. Two weeks later, she came to see me again, only this time she was accompanied by a tall, blonde, handsome man. She had met him on the way to work and later found out that he had just started a new job where she worked. She met him two days after casting the spell. She was over the moon, beaming from ear to ear. I kept pulling her leg as he was at least ten years younger than her, but she told me that's what she had asked for . . . a younger man. Call it fate, coincidence . . . I like to call it magic!

Moon Spell

If you were born under a full moon and you are down on luck you can call upon the Moon Goddess Diana to help you. You can call upon Diana three times only. There are three things that you must never ask for: destruction, power or death. These will not be granted.

Gaze up at the moon while saying the following;

> Moon, Moon, beautiful moon
> Brighter than any star,
> Goddess of light and love;
> Diana if it may be,
> Pray bring fortune unto me.

The spell must be carried out in between the new moons, which occur every thirty days. If Diana has heard what you asked of her, and if she has granted your wish, the coins in your pocket will have magically doubled, or a hare will cross your path before sunrise.

Star Spell

On a clear night open your window and look at the brightest star to the north while repeating these words. Wish very softly to yourself, and you shall obtain what you desire.

> Star light, star bright, very first star I have seen tonight,
> Wish I may, Wish I might,
> Have the wish I wish tonight. . .

LUCKY CHARMS

People wear or carry all manner of things, from a bent silver coin to a rabbit's foot, which they are convinced bring them good luck. The object itself, whatever it may be, is irrelevant, it's the power, faith and belief of the owner which make the charm lucky. I can fully understand this, as I always wear a crystal around my neck. I only ever remove it to wash, and I never leave the house without it. In fact, I wore it during my last operation!

My grandfather Jubal always carried a potato in his pocket, much to my grandmother's annoyance, especially on wash day, not for luck, but as a charm against rheumatism.

My sister always carries with her a silver bangle set with a single stone of Blue John. She only ever wears it on a Saturday, the reason being that Saturday is the seventh day of the week, and seven is her lucky number.

20 OF THE MOST POPULAR GOOD LUCK CHARMS

Usually worn around the neck as a pendant, set in a ring, or attached to a keyring and carried to bring good luck.

Beetle	Birth Stone
Cat	Clover
Coral	Cricket
Dice	Dog
Hammer	Horn of Life
Locket containing Soil	Pyramid
Rabbit's Foot	Salt (worn around the neck in a small glass bottle)
Shoe	Silver Coin
Toad	Three Brass Monkeys
Wheel of Life	Wishing Well

HALLOWEEN SPELLS

Hallow's Eve Spell

To eat an apple on Hallow's Eve seated alone before a mirror by candlelight is a very old spell, by means of which a girl seeks to see her future husband. If she is to marry, her sweetheart will come behind her and look into the mirror over her shoulder. She must continue eating the apple, blow out the candle, and on no account turn her head until the face has faded in the mirror.

Hallow's Eve Spell to Protect Horses

In Sweden, oats are touched with a hazel bough before being given to the horses to protect them from the evil eye. The hazel nuts (Corylus Auellana), when eaten, make their owner invisible. The nuts were also used for divination on Nutcrack Night, on All Hallow's Eve. On Halloween farmers used to 'bless' their cattle with black hellebore (Helleborus Niger) to protect them from falling under any enchantment. They scattered the herb around the stable, and burnt the powdered herb in a lantern which was hung outside.

Halloween Spell

At midnight on Halloween go to the wod pile and pull out the first stick handy. If the stick is smooth, the man you will marry will be young. If straight and even, he will be kind and gentle. If knotty, he will be violent. If bent and withered, he will be a bad tempered old man!

Thread and Spool

This spell must be done on halloween night before the moon fades. This is a very old country spell that requries courage. Go out into the woods holding the end of the thread in your left hand, throw the spool as far as you can into the darkness. A gentle pull will let you know that someone is there. Advance into the darkness, winding the end of the thread around your wedding finger until you see your lover with the spool in his hand. No words must pass, and no one must know about the spell until you are wed!

To Discover who will be the First to Marry

Put four cups of the same size on a round table. In one cup, place a ring, in another, a coin; and in another a sprig of orange blossom or heather, leaving the last cup empty. Those who wish to take part are blindfolded and must walk slowly three times around the table, then touch one of the cups. The first person to touch the cup containing the orange blossom or heather will be the first to wed. Anyone selecting the cup with the coin will never know want; the cup with the ring represents devoted love; the empty cup a single life.

To Ascertain if your Lover is True

Select a letter or card from your sweetheart, especially one which contains a particularly passionate and important declaration. Fold it nine times, then pin the folds together. Place the letter in your lefthand glove, and slip it under your pillow.

If that night you dream of silver, gems, glass, castles or clear water, your love is true and his declarations are genuine. If you dream of linen, storms, fire, wood, flowers, or that he is saluting you, he is false and has been deceiving you.*

To Discover what Kind of Man you will Marry

There is a curious old custom which ordains that girls go in couples to a cabbage patch and there blindfold themselves. Each pair then hold hands and wander about until they find a cabbage stalk, which they pull up.

If the stalk is long, their husbands will be tall; if it is stumpy, their husbands will be short; a crooked stalk indicates a man crooked in mind and body; a soft stalk, a husband who will be weak-willed; a hard stalk, a strong, self-willed man. Earth clinging to the roots of the stalk is a sign of wealth, while a clean stalk indicates poverty.*

Name Spell

This is a spell for a woman to find out the initials of the man she is to marry. In my grandmother's day, this spell was carried out under the light of the moon, in the well at the bottom of the garden past the woodpile.

Cut 26 squares from a piece of stiff cardboard. Write a letter of the alphabet on each square. Before going to bed, place the 26 squares in a bath of water, face down. In the morning the letters that have turned the right side up are the initials of the

---

* Taken from *The Complete Book of Fortune*, published by Chatto & Windus.

man you are to marry. If more than six letters turn up, this is a bad omen and the spell should be done a second time.

Loving Spoons

This spell is to find out whether you will marry and be happy, enter marriage and regret it, or remain single.

Girls pair up in couples and are blindfolded and bound together by the wrist. No matter how many people are taking part in this game, only nine spoons are used. The spoons are spread out on the floor. Each couple must crawl around on the floor in complete darkness and find a spoon. Once all the spoons have been found, the blindfolds are removed and the wrists untied.

If you picked up one spoon, your married life will be a lonely one. If two spoons, you will be happy and loved. If three, the marriage will be an unhappy one, filled with anger, tension and excessive arguments. Four spoons signifies divorce and a second marriage. Unlucky is the girl who doesn't find a spoon: she will never marry.

LOVE SPELLS

Love Bath

An invigorating bath to make a woman desirable, irresistible, and to ensure that the course of love runs smoothly in the right direction.

You Will Need
A handful of rosemary sprigs
1 cup of thyme leaves
2 tablespoons of powdered orris root
2 tablespoons of powdered lovage root
1 pint of soft water

Steep the rosemary and the thyme in a china or earthenware jug filled with boiling water; cover with a plate or saucer and leave to stand for 20–25 minutes. Then strain. Add the orris root and the lovage a little at a time, using a sieve. Stir well, add to bath water while still hot.

Loving Cup

This potion has magical qualities to ensure true love forever, to those who drink it.

You Will Need
1 handful of fresh elder flowers
2 tablespoons of virgin honey
1 pint of dry white wine
4 tablespoons of rosewater

First remove the stalks and any marked flowers. Rinse well in a sieve under cold water. Put into a china cup or bowl, drip the honey over the flowers, then pour over the wine. Cover the container with a lid or saucer and allow to steep for 6 hours. Strain with a fine sieve then stir in the rosewater. Now that the potion is ready, pour into a glass and both drink from it at the same time to make the course of love run true forever.

Love Charms

This charm is to be worn on the first date, before the first kiss. The herb that is to be used for this spell (lovage) must be picked in between the new moons, which occur every thirty days. Gather a little of the herb early in the morning after the dew has dried. Put the herb into a small round bag made from muslin. Either pin this close to your heart or wear it around the neck. If your man is taken with the pleasant aromatic smell, it will drive him wild with lust and passion!

Snake root, wrapped in muslin and carried in a pocket, will increase one's sexuality and arouse those of the opposite sex. Catmint, when worn around the neck on a piece of string, will arouse passion and certain physical powers. Rosemary, when worn by a woman will attract men and open all hearts. Sweet basil, when carried by a man, will strengthen his willpower and help to mellow his temper!

Love Meal

In the book *Secrets of Albertus Magnus* on the virtues of herbs, stones, and certain beasts, periwinkle is used as an aphrodisiac. 'Perwynke when it is beate unto pouder with worms of ye earth wrapped about it, and with an herbe called houslyke, it induceth love between man and wyfe if it bee used in their meales.'

In other words, take a handful of periwinkle, wrap earth worms around it, then beat to a powder. Mash together with houseleek, add to a meal and eat. This will induce love and passion between man and wife.

This is a very old spell, one that I do not recommend. However, I have added it merely for fun!

Love Pillow

Place this delightful scented pillow underneath your lover's head when he is asleep. He will dream of you and you only. Once you have won his love, the pillow must be burnt.

You Will Need
1 large cup of red rose petals
1 cup of honeysuckle flowers
1 tablespoon of powdered orris root
2 tablespoons of allspice
2 tablespoons of oil of pine (for a young man)
2 tablespoons of oil of musk (for an older man)
A lock of your hair

Dry the rose petals and honeysuckle flowers then put into a container. Sprinkle the herbs with the orris root, then mix together using your hands. Add the allspice, then leave in a warm dark place for 1 week. Stir the mixture gently every other day. Once ready for use, add either the pine or musk oil and shake once more. Sew into a small pillow made from muslin, not forgetting to place in the pillow a cutting of your hair.

Love Potion

It is an old Chinese belief that coriander seeds hold the power to induce love between a man and a woman. The seeds are also said to possess the power of immortality.

Crush a small handful of the seeds and add to a glass of wine, stir well, repeating the following 3 times:

> Warm seed, love run strong,
> Warm heart, let us never part.

Use a sweet white wine if you are young lovers, if mature select a good 'mature' red wine. The wine must be drunk warm, and from the same glass, and passion will be aroused!

Return to Me

In old folklore salt represents life. One should never throw salt away, as by doing so you are throwing away life itself, which is far too short as it is! However, salt is used in this spell to return the heart of a lover back to you. A woman who wishes to win back the heart and love of a man who has turned away from her must throw a pinch of salt into the fire for 9 mornings, saying as she does so:

> It is not the salt I mean to burn
> But my love's heart I mean to turn,
> Wishing him neither joy nor sleep,
> Till he comes back his trust to keep.

If, after nine mornings, your lover hasn't returned, take 12 pins and place in a dish containing slat, powdered rosemary, and a photograph of your lover. Set alight the dish at midnight, seated before a red burning candle. Repeat the following lines until the candle has completely burnt down to the wick.

> Flames of salt, return to me,
> Smoke of rosemary, remember me,
> Pins of fire, prick the heart,
> Return to me and never depart.

Once the dish has burnt, allow to cool before picking up the pins. Always leave a crooked pin in the dish. If you pick it up, you will 'pick up' sorrow.

To Open Hearts

Always carry with you a sprig of fresh rosemary, as rosemary brings love and it is the key to open the hearts of all men.

> Let this rosemary, this flower of men,
> Be a sign of your wisdom, love and loyalty,
> To be carried not only in the hand, but also
> In the heart. . .